Table of Contents

WOKE REVOLUTION

How Woke Ideology and Socialist Thinking Are Reshaping America

Billy J Riggs

ISBN: 9798230766216

Chapter 1

INTRODUCTION

Woke is a term that has become deeply embedded in contemporary cultural and political discourse, often used to describe a heightened awareness of social injustices, particularly those related to race, gender, and other forms of systemic oppression. To fully understand what it means to be "woke," it is essential to explore both the origins of the term and how its meaning has evolved over time.

Origins of the Term "Woke"

The term woke originally emerged from Black American slang vernacular where it simply functioned as the past tense of the verb wake. In this context, woke was used to describe someone who is awake or alert. However, by the mid-20th century, the term began to acquire a metaphorical sense. It was first recorded in this sense in a 1962 New York Times article by African American writer William Melvin Kelley, who used it in an article titled "If You're Woke You Dig It," discussing Black slang in Harlem. Here, woke meant being aware of the social, political, and racial dynamics affecting Black communities.

The concept of waking up to a deeper understanding of systemic injustice became more explicitly linked to social activism and consciousness during the Civil Rights Movement of the 1960s. The phrase "stay woke" was used to encourage Black Americans to remain vigilant and aware of the systemic racism and oppression they faced daily. It was a call to consciousness that also suggested an urgency to act against injustice.

Evolution and Popularization

For decades, the term woke remained primarily within Black communities as a term for being socially and politically aware. However, the term began to gain broader cultural significance in the 2010s, largely through the influence of social media. The phrase "stay woke" gained traction following the rise of the Black Lives Matter movement, which emerged in response to perceived police brutality and systemic racism, particularly after the killing of Trayvon Martin in 2012 and Michael Brown in 2014. The term was popularized through social media hashtags, music, and political activism, where it was used to signify awareness and resistance against injustice.

One notable moment in this popularization came with the 2016 song *Redbone* by Childish Gambino (Donald Glover), which included the refrain "Stay woke." The song's success helped to cement woke in the broader Black culture lexicon, tying it to the themes of awareness and vigilance against the dangers facing marginalized communities.

What Does It Mean to Be Woke?

Being woke originally meant being aware of social injustices, particularly those affecting Black communities, and understanding the ways in which these injustices are rooted in systemic oppression. It implied a heightened consciousness of the political and social realities that shape people's lives, often including the perception of privilege and the ways it interacts with race, class, gender, sexuality, and other identities.

Over time, the concept of wokeness has expanded beyond its original context to include awareness of a broad range of social justice issues. To be woke today often means being attuned to a variety of intersecting oppressions, including sexism, ableism, homophobia, transphobia, xenophobia, and economic inequality. It signifies a commitment to political leftist policies advocating for marginalized communities and challenging the systems that perpetuate inequality.

Contemporary Usage and Controversy

As the term woke entered mainstream discourse, its meaning began to shift, and it has since become a contested term. Many progressive activists and thinkers still use woke positively, viewing it as shorthand for social awareness, empathy, and a commitment to social justice. To them, being woke is a badge of honor that reflects a conscious effort to understand and dismantle societal inequities.

However, as the term gained popularity, it also began to attract criticism and satire. For some, particularly on the political right, woke has become a pejorative term used to describe what they perceive as excessive political correctness, virtue signaling, or performative activism. In this context, woke is often associated with a perceived overemphasis on identity politics or an insistence on purity that is seen as divisive or counterproductive.

In Earl Nightingale's, *The Greatest Secret*, the phrase "human society is not programmed to prevent the strong from winning, but to prevent the weak from losing" reflects a fundamental tension at the heart of many societal debates surrounding woke ideology. At its core, this phrase speaks to the balance between competition and compassion, between meritocracy and equality, and between individual success and collective responsibility. Woke ideology, with its emphasis on social justice, equity, and inclusion, seeks to address historical and systemic injustices that have marginalized certain groups, but it also raises questions about how society balances these competing values.

Preventing the Weak from Losing: The Essence of Woke Ideology

<hr>

Woke ideology is often rooted in the belief that society has historically favored the strong, those with power, monetary privilege, and access to resources, at the expense of the weak those who have been marginalized, oppressed, or disadvantaged by systemic biases. From this perspective, woke ideology seeks to create a more equitable society by preventing the weak from losing, ensuring that those who have been traditionally taught they were disadvantaged are given benefits and resources similar to those who decided to succeed and thrive regardless of their family or cultural history.

Addressing Historical Inequities

Woke ideologies argue that many of the disparities seen today are not merely the result of individual failings or lack of effort but are rooted in deep-seated historical injustices. For example, systemic racism, gender discrimination, and economic inequality are perceived as structural barriers that have prevented marginalized groups and individuals from accessing opportunities available to others. To prevent the weak from losing, woke advocates call for policies and practices that actively redress these perceived imbalances such as affirmative action, reparations, or redistributive justice.

Leveling the Playing Field

The idea of preventing the weak from losing aligns with efforts to level the playing field. In education, for example, woke ideologies promote diverse curricula that reflect multiple perspectives, culturally responsive teaching practices, and equity in school funding. The goal is to ensure that all students, regardless of their background, have an equal chance to succeed. This approach extends to other areas, such as employment practices and housing policies, where initiatives like DEI (Diversity, Equity, and Inclusion) aim to remove barriers that have historically disadvantaged certain groups.

Mandating Collective Responsibility

Woke ideologies emphasize a collective responsibility to address social injustices. This means that society as a whole has an obligation to ensure that the weak do not lose, even if it requires significant changes to existing systems or redistributing resources. Historically this has been viewed as socialism. This approach often involves rethinking traditional metrics of success, such as economic growth or competitive achievement, and instead focusing on social welfare, equity, and the well-being of all members of society.

Unintended Consequences of Woke Ideology

While the phrase highlights the need to protect the weak, it also implicitly acknowledges the importance of not preventing the strong from winning. Herein lies a core tension: how can society uplift the disadvantaged without unfairly limiting the opportunities of those who are already succeeding?

Woke ideology often critiques the notion of meritocracy, arguing that it is a myth that masks deeper systemic biases. However, some critics argue that certain woke policies might inadvertently penalize those who are perceived as strong, those who have achieved success through hard work, talent, or innovation. For example, debates over college admissions policies or hiring practices that prioritize diversity can lead to concerns about reverse discrimination, where individuals from groups historically perceived as privileged may feel they are being unfairly penalized.

There is an ongoing debate about how to balance equity with excellence. If too much emphasis is placed on preventing the weak from losing, some argue that it may discourage individual initiative, creativity, and the pursuit of excellence. For instance, policies that seek to reduce disparities in outcomes might lower standards or reduce incentives for high performance. Critics worry that such policies could weaken institutions' ability to reward merit, thereby limiting opportunities for innovation and progress.

The phrase suggests that society should prevent the weak from losing without necessarily handicapping the strong. However, in practice, implementing woke policies often involves difficult trade-offs. Some individuals and groups often perceive these policies as a threat to their own opportunities or achievements, leading to polarization and resistance. This tension is evident in debates over free speech on college campuses, where efforts to create safe and inclusive spaces for marginalized groups are sometimes seen as infringing on the rights of others.

To fully embrace the idea that society should prevent the weak from losing while allowing the strong to win, there must be a balance between compassion and competition, between fairness and freedom. In its current form, woke ideology mandates that society reimagine its social contract, to find new ways to ensure that all individuals have the chance to succeed and placing that responsibility on those with ambition and the drive to succeed.

Effective woke policies allegedly aim to provide equal opportunities, rather than equal outcomes. For example, providing quality education, healthcare, and economic opportunities to all to help prevent the weak from losing, without penalizing those who have excelled. Ensuring a level playing field where everyone has access to the resources needed to succeed is a way to balance the two principles.

A balanced approach should recognize the importance of resilience, self-determination, and growth. Supporting the weak should not mean creating dependency or eliminating competition. Rather, it should involve creating environments where all individuals are empowered to develop their strengths and reach their full potential. This approach acknowledges that while not everyone starts from the same place, everyone should have the opportunity to thrive.

Redefining Success

W oke ideologies seek to redefine success to include social well-being, justice, and equity, rather than just economic or individual achievement. Ideally, a society that prevents the weak from losing, while allowing the strong to win, is one that values both collective progress and personal accomplishment. It is a society that finds strength in diversity, resilience in compassion, and wisdom in fairness.

An understanding that human society is not programmed to prevent the strong from winning, but to prevent the weak from losing offers a lens through which to view the impact and challenges of woke ideologies. It highlights the need for a balanced approach that promotes fairness and justice for all, while recognizing the value of competition, innovation, and individual excellence. As society grapples with these complexities, the conversation around woke ideologies will continue to evolve, reflecting deeper questions about what it means to be just, fair, and free.

Chapter 2

The Global Influence of Woke Ideologies

Woke ideologies centered around social justice, equity, diversity, and inclusion, have been adopted to varying degrees by different countries, influencing their governance, policies, and social direction. The adoption of these ideologies is often shaped by each country's historical, political, and economic context.

For example, several countries have incorporated these ideologies to varying degrees, influencing their social policies, taxation, and inflation rates. In contrast, Russia, with its more authoritarian governance, has largely resisted woke principles. Let's take a look at ten different countries, each with a distinct form of government, that have incorporated woke principles and examine how these ideologies have shaped their economic policies, inflationary trends, and societal development.

Canada: A Capitalist Democracy

Canada, under the leadership of Prime Minister Justin Trudeau, has become known for its progressive stance on social justice issues. Trudeau's government has embraced woke ideologies, advocating for diversity, equity, and inclusion across multiple facets of Canadian society.

Canada has implemented several policies aimed at promoting diversity and inclusion. The government has established gender quotas in federal appointments, promoted bilingualism, and enacted laws that protect the rights of LGBTQ+ communities. For example, the passage of Bill C-16 in 2017 added gender identity and expression as protected categories under Canadian human rights law.

Canada's reconciliation efforts with its Indigenous peoples reflect woke principles. The government has acknowledged historical wrongs, such as the residential school system, and committed to the Truth and Reconciliation Commission's recommendations, including addressing land claims and improving access to essential services.

These policies have garnered both support and criticism. Advocates argue that Canada's woke approach has made the country more inclusive and just, whereas critics claim it has led to excessive political correctness and polarization. Economically, Canada has balanced these policies with its capitalist framework, but some argue that these efforts strain public resources and create tensions around national identity.

Taxation and Government Spending

Canada has implemented various social policies aligned with woke ideologies, such as increased spending on social services, healthcare, and initiatives aimed at improving diversity and equity. This spending has required a progressive tax system where higher earners pay a greater percentage of their income in taxes to support woke policies.

The Trudeau government has also introduced specific taxes to fund climate initiatives and social programs, such as a federal carbon tax. While these taxes aim to reduce emissions and support green energy, they have also been a point of contention for some provinces and businesses that see them as a government mandated cost burden. The costs associated with progressive social programs have contributed modestly to inflation, but broader global economic factors have had a more significant impact.

The impact of woke policies on Canada's economy is mixed. On one hand, policies promoting diversity and inclusion have arguably enhanced social cohesion and increased participation in the labor market. On the other hand, some businesses argue that increased taxes and regulatory costs associated with these policies have dampened competitiveness. Overall, Canada's economy has remained relatively stable, but the long-term effects of these policies are still unfolding.

New Zealand: A Capitalist Welfare State

New Zealand, under the leadership of former Prime Minister Jacinda Ardern, has positioned itself as a progressive beacon, emphasizing social justice, gender equality, and environmentalism.

Ardern's government took significant steps to promote gender equality, implementing policies such as paid parental leave, equal pay legislation, and gender-balanced political representation. Her administration was also vocal about the importance of mental health, social welfare, and addressing domestic violence.

New Zealand has emphasized the recognition of Maori rights and culture, incorporating the Maori language and traditions into national life. The government has also pursued a more inclusive narrative by integrating Maori values and perspectives into legislation and public policy.

New Zealand's adoption of woke ideologies has reinforced its image as an inclusive, forward-thinking society. While these policies have largely been seen positively, with many New Zealanders appreciating the focus on equity and diversity, critics argue that such policies have prioritized symbolic gestures over substantive economic and social reforms.

Taxation and Government Spending

New Zealand has maintained a welfare state model with robust social services, which aligns with many woke ideologies. The Ardern government expanded social spending on healthcare, education, and welfare programs, while also introducing policies aimed at promoting gender equality and reducing poverty.

The funding for these programs has come from a mix of increased direct taxes, such as income and corporate taxes, and indirect taxes, like the Goods and Services Tax (GST). The government has also increased spending on mental health and environmental initiatives, which align with a socially progressive agenda.

Recent policy shifts, including increased social spending and regulatory changes, have introduced new costs for businesses. Inflation in New Zealand has generally been low. However, inflation has recently increased significantly, driven by global factors like supply chain disruptions and domestic factors like housing shortages and increased demand for services.

New Zealand's adoption of woke ideologies has generally supported a stable economy, but with some trade-offs. Progressive policies have contributed to greater social equity and cohesion. However, they have also led to significantly higher taxes and regulatory burdens that negatively impact small businesses and lower-income groups. The long-term economic impacts of these policies, particularly in balancing social equity with economic growth, are still being debated.

Sweden: A Democratic Socialist State

Sweden, known for its robust welfare state, has embraced woke ideologies that align with its long-standing commitment to social justice, human rights, and equality.

Sweden has pioneered gender equality, introducing generous parental leave policies that encourage both parents to take time off, and promoting gender balance in corporate boards. The country has also passed laws aimed at closing the gender pay gap and preventing gender discrimination.

Sweden's liberal immigration policies are reflective of woke ideals of inclusivity and humanitarianism. Sweden has welcomed refugees and asylum seekers, particularly from conflict zones, and has made efforts to integrate them into Swedish society through language programs, housing, and employment initiatives.

While Sweden's woke policies have promoted gender equity and human rights, they have also led to debates about social cohesion and economic sustainability. The influx of refugees has sparked discussions about the capacity of Sweden's welfare system to support newcomers without compromising the quality of services for citizens. Additionally, many Swedes express concern over cultural integration and national identity.

Taxation and Government Spending

Sweden's democratic socialist model has long embraced progressive social policies that align with woke ideologies, such as gender equality, inclusive immigration policies, and robust welfare programs. These programs are funded by one of the highest tax rates in the world, including high-income, corporate, and value-added taxes.

Sweden's high-tax model supports extensive public services, from healthcare and education to childcare and parental leave. The government's policies are designed to redistribute wealth and promote social equity, which aligns closely with woke ideologies.

Inflation in Sweden has generally remained low. However, recent economic challenges, such as the impact of the pandemic and supply chain disruptions, have led to higher inflation rates.

Sweden's approach to woke ideologies has led to a high degree of social equity and strong public services, but it has also come with high taxes and significant government intervention in the economy. While the country has maintained strong economic fundamentals, some argue that the high tax burden and regulatory environment has significantly limited entrepreneurial activity and private sector growth.

The Netherlands: A Liberal Capitalist Democracy

The Netherlands, with its tradition of liberal values, has embraced woke ideologies in various forms, from LGBTQ+ rights to climate change initiatives.

The Netherlands was the first country in the world to legalize same-sex marriage in 2001, and it continues to be a leader in LGBTQ+ rights, with extensive protections against discrimination and a strong stance on inclusivity.

Woke ideologies in the Netherlands have also driven ambitious climate policies. The Dutch government has implemented measures to reduce carbon emissions, promote renewable energy, and encourage sustainable practices. For example, the Netherlands has set goals to eliminate gas heating in homes by 2050 and is investing heavily in wind and solar energy.

While the Netherlands has been praised for its progressive stance on social justice and environmental issues, it also faces challenges. The country's liberal immigration policies, for example, have led to debates about integration, social services, and national identity. Additionally, the cost of transitioning to sustainable energy has sparked discussions about economic feasibility and the impact on low-income communities.

Taxation and Government Spending

The Netherlands combines a liberal capitalist economy with progressive social policies, such as LGBTQ+ rights, climate initiatives, and social welfare programs. These policies are funded through a relatively high tax regime, including income taxes, corporate taxes, and value-added taxes.

The Dutch government has implemented taxes aimed at promoting sustainability, such as carbon taxes and incentives for renewable energy adoption. These measures are part of the country's broader strategy to combat climate change and promote social justice.

Inflation in the Netherlands has generally been low, but recent years have seen significant increases due to rising energy costs, housing prices, and global supply chain issues. The government's commitment to climate action and social equity has introduced increased costs, but these have generally been balanced by economic growth.

The Netherlands' progressive policies have contributed to a stable and inclusive society, but they have also sparked debates about the economic cost of such policies, particularly concerning energy prices and taxation. The Dutch approach reflects a balance between liberal economic policies and social progressivism, attempting to maintain economic growth while addressing social justice issues.

South Africa: A Capitalist Democracy

South Africa's post-apartheid government has been influenced by woke ideologies, particularly in addressing racial inequality and promoting reconciliation.

In an effort to address historical injustices, South Africa has implemented policies such as Black Economic Empowerment and affirmative action in hiring and education. These policies aim to uplift Black South Africans by promoting representation and economic opportunities.

Woke ideologies have also influenced South Africa's land reform policies, which seek to address the historical dispossession of land from Black South Africans. The government has proposed the socialist approach of expropriation without compensation as a means to redistribute land more equitably.

While these policies aim to prevent the weak from losing and address systemic injustices, they have also been controversial. Critics argue that affirmative action and Black Economic Empowerment policies have lead to inefficiencies, reverse discrimination, and corruption. Land reform, while addressing historical grievances, has faced challenges related to implementation and concerns about investor confidence and agricultural productivity.

Taxation and Government Spending

As mentioned earlier, South Africa's government has adopted policies aimed at redressing historical injustices, such as Black Economic Empowerment, land reform, and affirmative action in hiring and education. These policies are intended to promote economic inclusion and address the legacy of apartheid.

The cost of these social justice policies has been significant, requiring increased government spending and creating new taxes and regulatory requirements for businesses. South Africa has relatively high taxes, particularly for individuals and businesses, to fund social programs and address inequality.

South Africa's GDP growth has been relatively sluggish over the past two decades, averaging around 1-2%. The economy faces challenges, including high unemployment, income inequality, and political instability, which many argue have been exacerbated by woke policies.

Inflation in South Africa has generally been higher than in other countries. Inflationary pressures are partly due to structural issues in the economy, such as energy shortages and supply constraints, as well as the costs associated with social justice policies.

South Africa's adoption of woke ideologies through policies aimed at redressing past injustices has had mixed economic results. While these policies have helped to promote social equity and inclusion, they have also led to economic challenges, such as reduced foreign investment, slower growth, and higher inflation. Critics argue that these policies have created an uncertain business environment, while supporters believe they are necessary to achieve long-term social stability and justice.

Great Britain: A Capitalist Democracy

In the United Kingdom, woke ideologies have been evident in various social and political initiatives, particularly under the Labour Party and progressive factions within the Conservative Party. Issues like racial equality, LGBTQ+ rights, gender parity, and climate action have become focal points in public discourse.

The UK has implemented several woke-inspired policies, such as mandating gender pay gap reporting for large employers, introducing diversity quotas for boards, and expanding hate crime legislation. There is also a significant emphasis on decolonizing the curriculum in schools and universities, aiming to reflect a more inclusive historical perspective.

Impact on Inflation and Taxation

To support progressive policies, such as increased social spending and green initiatives, there have been pushes for higher taxes on corporations and the wealthy. For example, discussions about a "Green New Deal" in the UK Parliament have included potential increases in environmental taxes, aimed at reducing carbon emissions.

The direct impact of woke ideologies on inflation is not difficult to quantify. The costs associated with implementing diversity and inclusion programs and shifting to sustainable energy sources have contributed to public spending. This spending, combined with broader economic challenges like Brexit, supply chain disruptions, and the COVID-19 pandemic, has contributed to recent inflationary pressures. The UK has seen inflation rates rise significantly in recent years, peaking at over 10% in 2022.

Woke ideologies have led to increased awareness of social justice issues in Britain, influencing public policy and corporate behavior. However, these changes have also sparked cultural debates and political polarization, particularly among those who view such policies as excessive or detrimental to free speech and traditional values.

Germany: A Social Market Economy

Germany, under its social market economy model, has embraced elements of woke ideologies, particularly in areas like gender equality, environmentalism, and immigration. The country has implemented policies aimed at fostering inclusivity, such as the Gender Pay Gap Act, which requires companies to report pay disparities, and the Gender Quota Law, mandating that a certain percentage of supervisory board positions be held by women.

Germany's response to immigration has also been influenced by woke ideologies, especially during Angela Merkel's tenure as Chancellor, when she adopted a welcoming stance towards refugees from conflict zones. This policy has been both lauded as a humanitarian approach and criticized for its economic and social implications.

Impact on Inflation and Taxation

Germany's adoption of progressive policies has led to moderate increases in taxes, particularly to support social programs and climate initiatives. For example, Germany introduced a carbon tax in 2021, aimed at reducing carbon emissions and funding the transition to renewable energy sources.

Inflation in Germany has been relatively stable over the past two decades but has recently increased due to global factors like supply chain disruptions and rising energy prices. The costs associated with integrating a large number of refugees and transitioning to sustainable energy have put additional pressure on public finances, contributing significantly to inflationary trends.

The adoption of woke ideologies in Germany has encouraged a more inclusive society and fostered a strong commitment to environmental sustainability. However, these policies have also generated debates about economic costs, social integration, and the limits of progressive reforms, particularly in the context of economic challenges like inflation and the energy crisis.

Russia: An Authoritarian State

Unlike Western European nations, Russia has largely resisted woke ideologies, particularly under the leadership of President Vladimir Putin. The Russian government has positioned itself as a defender of "traditional values" against what it perceives as the moral and cultural decline of the West. This stance has included passing laws against "gay propaganda," restricting LGBTQ+ rights, and cracking down on feminist and human rights organizations.

Russia's resistance to woke ideologies has been tied to its broader geopolitical strategy, presenting itself as an alternative to Western liberal democracies. The government has framed woke ideologies as a threat to Russian identity, culture, and national sovereignty similar to how it framed Christianity throughout most of the twentieth century.

Impact on Inflation and Taxation

Russia's tax policies have not been significantly influenced by woke ideologies. Instead, they focus on maintaining a stable economic environment, particularly for the wealthy and large state-owned enterprises. The country has a flat tax rate of 13% for most citizens and has been cautious about introducing progressive taxes that could be perceived as promoting equity in the way Western countries do.

Inflation in Russia has been driven primarily by external factors, such as international sanctions, oil price fluctuations, and the geopolitical situation, rather than domestic social policies. Recent inflation rates have been volatile, particularly following the invasion of Ukraine and subsequent economic sanctions from Western countries, which have led to significant price increases and economic contraction.

Russia's rejection of woke ideologies has reinforced its authoritarian governance model and appeal to conservative values. However, this stance has isolated Russia from much of the Western world, exacerbating economic challenges and limiting social progress on issues like gender equality and LGBTQ+ rights.

France: A Capitalist Republic

France has a complex relationship with woke ideologies, blending elements of social justice with a strong emphasis on secularism and national identity. The French government has promoted policies that address racial and gender inequality, such as initiatives to improve diversity in public and private sectors and laws to close the gender pay gap.

However, France has also been critical of some aspects of woke culture, particularly those that are perceived to challenge the French Republican values of secularism and universalism. President Emmanuel Macron, for instance, has criticized what he calls "American woke culture" and its perceived threats to French identity and unity.

Impact on Inflation and Taxation

France has a progressive tax system that funds its extensive welfare state, which includes universal healthcare, education, and social safety nets. The country has introduced various taxes aimed at promoting equity and social justice, such as wealth taxes, carbon taxes, and higher corporate taxes for large companies.

Inflation has recently increased due to global supply chain disruptions, energy prices, and the economic impact of the COVID-19 pandemic. While woke policies themselves have not directly driven inflation, the cost of implementing social programs and green initiatives have increased inflationary pressures and are expected to continue to do so over time.

France's adoption of woke ideologies has led to increased awareness and action on social justice issues, but it has also sparked debates about national identity, secularism, and cultural unity. The economic impact of these policies has been significant, through higher taxes and some inflationary pressures, but the country continues to balance progressive reforms with its unique cultural and political context.

The United States: A Democratic Republic

Woke ideologies, centered on social justice, diversity, equity, and inclusion, have significantly shaped the social and political landscape of the United States over the past decade. These ideologies have influenced various aspects of American society, including government policies, corporate practices, education, and cultural discourse. The rise of woke ideologies has also had significant economic ramifications, affecting inflation rates, taxation policies, and broader economic dynamics.

Woke ideologies have permeated the cultural and political fabric of the United States, driving conversations around race, gender, sexuality, and systemic inequality. The term "woke," originally used to denote awareness of racial and social injustices, has evolved to encompass a broader range of progressive causes, from LGBTQ+ rights and gender equality to environmental justice and anti-capitalist critiques.

The adoption of woke ideologies has led to a heightened focus on diversity, equity, and inclusion (DEI) initiatives across various sectors, including corporate America, education, entertainment, and government institutions. Corporations have increasingly adopted DEI policies, often appointing Chief Diversity Officers and implementing training programs to address "unconscious" bias, racial inequities, and promote inclusive workplace cultures.

In politics, woke ideologies have been embraced by progressive factions within the Democratic Party, influencing policies related to healthcare, education, criminal justice reform, and climate change. Movements like Black Lives Matter (BLM), #MeToo, and other grassroots campaigns have gained significant traction, driving legislative and policy changes at the local, state, and federal levels.

Woke ideologies have driven significant policy shifts, such as the push for police reform, reparations for slavery, expanded civil rights protections for LGBTQ+ individuals, and climate action. For example, in 2020, President Joe Biden signed executive orders promoting racial equity, including ending contracts with private prisons and advancing housing equity.

The influence of woke ideologies has also been visible in the cultural sphere, from changes in school curricula to reflect diverse perspectives other than Christianity, to shifts in corporate marketing and advertising strategies that emphasize inclusivity. Companies and institutions have increasingly been held accountable by consumers, employees, and the public to align their values and practices with these ideals regardless of economic impact.

However, the rise of woke ideologies has also led to backlash and polarization, particularly among conservative and moderate groups. Critics argue that woke policies undermine free speech, foster a culture of censorship, and impose ideological conformity. The debate over issues like critical race theory in schools and corporate DEI training has become a flashpoint in national politics, highlighting deep cultural divides.

Impact on Inflation Rates and Economic Dynamics

———

The direct economic impact of woke ideologies on inflation is challenging to quantify, as inflation is driven by various factors, including monetary policy, supply chain disruptions, energy prices, and global economic conditions. However, some aspects of woke policies have directly contributed to inflationary pressures.

For example, environmental policies aligned with woke ideologies, such as carbon taxes, stricter environmental regulations, and investments in green energy, may increase costs for businesses, which can then be passed on to consumers. Similarly, increased spending on social programs and equity initiatives can contribute to government deficits, potentially leading to inflationary pressures.

In recent years, inflation rates in the United States have surged, peaking at over 9% in 2022—the highest in four decades. While the primary drivers of this inflation have been factors like supply chain disruptions, the COVID-19 pandemic, and government spending on the war in Ukraine, the costs associated with social and environmental policies may have added to the overall inflationary environment.

Woke ideologies have also impacted labor markets and wage dynamics. Efforts to raise the minimum wage, promote pay equity, and enforce fair labor practices have led to wage increases in many sectors. The push for a $15 minimum wage, for instance, has gained traction in many states and cities, driven by progressive activists and policymakers.

While higher wages can improve living standards for low-income workers, they may also increase costs for businesses, particularly small businesses, which may pass on these costs to consumers through higher prices, contributing to inflation. Some employers have also faced pressure to offer more generous benefits, such as paid family leave, healthcare, and childcare support, which may impact their overall cost structures.

Progressive Taxation and Redistribution

Woke ideologies have influenced the debate over taxation in the United States, with calls for higher taxes on the wealthy, corporations, and capital gains to fund social programs and reduce economic inequality. Progressive policymakers and activists have advocated for a wealth tax, increased corporate tax rates, and closing tax loopholes to ensure that the richest Americans and corporations pay their "fair share."

In 2021, the Biden administration proposed several tax reforms aimed at increasing revenue from high earners and corporations to fund infrastructure, education, and social programs. While not all proposed changes have been enacted, the direction of tax policy has shifted towards greater progressivity, reflecting the influence of woke ideologies on economic policy.

Woke ideologies have also led to increased scrutiny of corporate tax practices. Activists and policymakers have called for greater transparency and accountability regarding corporate tax payments, emphasizing the need to address tax avoidance and evasion by multinational corporations. This scrutiny has led to a renewed focus on reforming international tax rules and cracking down on profit-shifting to low-tax jurisdictions.

At the state and local levels, there have been efforts to implement taxes on specific industries or activities perceived as contributing to social or environmental harm, such as taxes on sugary drinks, plastic bags, and fossil fuels. These taxes reflect a broader trend towards using government policy to enforce social justice and environmental sustainability.

The impact of woke ideologies on the United States has been complex and multifaceted. On one hand, these ideologies have driven significant social change, promoting greater awareness of systemic inequalities and fostering more inclusive policies in government, education, and the private sector. They have encouraged a shift towards progressive taxation and increased scrutiny of corporate practices, reflecting a broader commitment to social justice and equity.

On the other hand, the economic impact of these ideologies has been mixed. While efforts to promote diversity, equity, and inclusion have contributed to social cohesion and improved workplace environments, they have also caused division between segments of the population who view them as excessive or counterproductive. The indirect costs associated with implementing progressive policies, combined with broader economic challenges, have contributed to debates about the balance between social justice and economic stability.

As the United States continues to navigate these challenges, the influence of woke ideologies will likely remain a central feature of its social and political landscape, shaping the country's direction in the years to come. The key question moving forward will be how to reconcile the goals of democratic socialism and the inherent economic realities of high inflation, increased taxation, and government control with the constitutional protections of a free society in a complex and rapidly changing world.

Summation

The adoption of woke ideologies across different types of governments demonstrates the global influence of social justice movements. In capitalist democracies like Canada and New Zealand, woke principles have driven progressive reforms, while in democratic socialist states like Sweden, these ideologies have reinforced long-standing commitments to equality and social welfare. However, each country faces its own unique challenges in balancing these ideals with economic sustainability, social cohesion, and public sentiment. As these nations continue to evolve, the debate over how to best implement woke ideologies in governance will likely remain a contentious topic.

Chapter 3

Woke Ideology and Politicians

Today, woke stands at a crossroads. For many, it remains an important term for understanding and articulating the need for social justice. It represents a call to action and awareness that challenges individuals to confront their own biases and the systemic inequalities that shape our world. However, its appropriation, redefinition, and politicization mean that it is also a term fraught with ambiguity and contention.

The debate over what it means to be woke reflects broader societal conflicts over how we understand and address issues of race, privilege, and social justice. Whether woke will continue to be a rallying cry for those committed to social progress, or whether it will lose its potency due to overuse, misunderstanding, and weaponization, remains to be seen.

The term woke has become a lightning rod in political discourse, often used by politicians to signal their stance on social and cultural issues. Let's take a look at a few notable examples of how politicians have used the term woke and how the general public has responded to its use:

Donald Trump (U.S. President Elect)

Donald Trump has frequently used the term woke in a pejorative sense to criticize progressive policies and cultural movements. For example, in 2021, Trump declared, "Everything woke turns to shit," during a rally in Arizona, implying that progressive policies or unaccountable social justice movements are harmful to the country.

Trump's use of woke was well-received by his base, who see it as a rejection of political correctness and an affirmation of traditional values. However, his use of the term has also been criticized by progressives, who view it as an attack on efforts to address systemic injustice and inequality.

Ron DeSantis (Governor of Florida)

———

Ron DeSantis has made opposition to wokeness a central theme of his political brand. He signed Florida's Stop WOKE Act in 2022, targeting workplace and school diversity training programs that claim to address systemic racism or privilege. He has frequently described Florida as "where woke goes to die," framing his policies as a stand against what he sees as overreach by progressive ideologies.

DeSantis's use of woke resonates with many conservatives who see it as a defense against what they perceive as left-wing cultural encroachment. However, it has sparked backlash from educators, activists, and many Democrats, who argue that his policies are an attack on free speech and educational freedom.

Ted Cruz (U.S. Senator)

Ted Cruz has used the term woke to criticize a variety of policies and cultural phenomena, ranging from corporate diversity initiatives to the U.S. military. In 2021, he tweeted that the U.S. military was "embracing woke culture" after a recruitment ad featured a female soldier. Cruz claimed that such wokeness made the military less effective compared to its adversaries.

Cruz's comments were met with a mixed reaction. His conservative followers generally supported his critique, viewing woke policies as weakening American institutions. On the other hand, many military members and veterans criticized Cruz for disparaging the armed forces, arguing that diversity and inclusion are strengths, not weaknesses.

Nikki Haley (Former U.S. Ambassador to the UN)

Nikki Haley has used woke as a critique against the Democratic Party and progressive activists, accusing them of pushing an extreme Socialist agenda. During her speeches, she has argued that wokeism is dividing America and undermining the country's founding principles.

Haley's use of woke aligns with other conservatives' critiques of progressive movements. While her stance resonates with conservative audiences, it has also been met with criticism by those who argue that such rhetoric ignores legitimate social justice concerns and attempts to delegitimize advocacy for equality.

Rishi Sunak (Prime Minister of the UK)

Rishi Sunak has also invoked the term woke in a negative context, especially in reference to educational content and cultural debates. In his 2023 Conservative Party Conference speech, Sunak criticized woke nonsense in the British education system, advocating for policies that reflect traditional values and common sense.

In the UK, Sunak's use of woke has received mixed responses. Some conservatives have applauded his stand against perceived overreach by progressives, while others, including some moderate conservatives, have expressed concern that such language might alienate younger voters and those more sympathetic to social justice causes.

Nancy Pelosi (Former Speaker of the House of Representatives)

As Speaker of the House, Nancy Pelosi has often aligned herself with progressive causes and policies that are associated with woke ideologies. While she hasn't frequently used the term woke itself in her public speeches, she has endorsed the principles of social justice and inclusion that the term often represents. For example, Pelosi has supported movements like Black Lives Matter and advocated for policies such as police reform, gender equality, and LGBTQ+ rights.

Pelosi's alignment with woke ideologies has helped her maintain strong ties with the progressive wing of the Democratic Party. By supporting policies like the George Floyd Justice in Policing Act, which aims to address police brutality and systemic racism, Pelosi has demonstrated her commitment to the values championed by woke movements. Additionally, she has pushed for legislation related to climate action, voting rights, and social equity, all of which are rooted in woke principles of equity and justice.

Pelosi's stance has energized progressive Democrats and grassroots activists, helping to secure the support of key constituencies. However, it has also attracted criticism from conservatives who argue that these policies are divisive or excessively focused on identity politics.

Barack Obama: (Former U.S. President)

Former President Barack Obama has been more critical of certain aspects of what he perceives as woke culture. In a 2019 summit, Obama warned against call-out culture, where people aggressively criticize others for perceived ideological purity or minor infractions. While he did not explicitly use the term woke during this speech, his comments were widely interpreted as a critique of some woke behaviors that he viewed as counterproductive.

Obama's comments reflect a more moderate or pragmatic approach within the Democratic Party. While he has consistently supported progressive causes such as racial equality, healthcare reform, and LGBTQ+ rights, Obama has emphasized the need for coalition-building and pragmatic politics. His critique of certain aspects of woke culture suggests a belief that overly rigid or extreme positions could alienate potential allies and hinder broader progressive goals.

Obama's stance has been influential in shaping debates within the Democratic Party. Many moderates and centrists have echoed his concerns, arguing that excessive focus on ideological purity can be polarizing and counterproductive. At the same time, some progressives have criticized his remarks as dismissive of legitimate grievances and social justice efforts.

Maxine Waters: (Former U.S. Representative)

———

Congresswoman Maxine Waters has been a vocal advocate for social justice and equality, often aligning herself with woke ideologies. While she may not frequently use the term woke itself, her political rhetoric and actions embody its principles. Waters has championed causes like racial justice, economic equity, and police reform, consistently advocating for marginalized communities.

Waters has used her platform to call for systemic change, such as advocating for police accountability and criticizing institutional racism. In response to incidents of police brutality, she has been outspoken in demanding justice and supporting movements like BLM. Her calls for retaliation and direct engagement with these issues are in line with woke principles of activism and awareness.

For example, in 2021, during the trial of Derek Chauvin for the murder of George Floyd, Waters urged protesters to "stay on the street" and "get more confrontational" if a guilty verdict was not delivered, which demonstrated her support for violent retaliation to achieve social justice.

Waters' strong advocacy has made her a prominent figure among progressive activists and communities of color. However, her rhetoric has also been polarizing, with critics accusing her of inciting violence or promoting radical policies.

Hillary Clinton

Hillary Clinton has generally avoided using the term woke in a direct sense but has engaged with the issues it represents, such as gender equality, LGBTQ+ rights, and racial justice. During her 2016 presidential campaign, Clinton supported policies that aligned with woke ideologies, including criminal justice reform, paid family leave, and increased diversity in leadership roles.

Clinton has positioned herself as a progressive leader who balances social justice with pragmatic governance. She has frequently spoken about systemic inequalities and the need for inclusive policies while also calling for a measured approach to achieving these goals. For example, Clinton has advocated for ending systemic racism and sexism but has emphasized the importance of working within existing political structures.

During her 2016 campaign, Clinton's efforts to reach out to progressive voters included embracing feminist and anti-racist rhetoric, advocating for gun control, and supporting progressive taxation and healthcare reform.

Clinton's approach has often been seen as an attempt to bridge the gap between progressives and moderates within the Democratic Party. While she has successfully mobilized many progressive voters, she has also faced criticism from both the left for not being progressive enough and the right for being too aligned with woke ideals.

Overall Impact

The use of woke ideologies by these politicians has both mobilized progressive constituencies and intensified political polarization in the U.S. Supporters argue that such advocacy helps address systemic inequalities and creates a fairer society. In contrast, opponents often contend that woke policies undermine free speech, promote divisiveness, and impose ideological conformity.

Politicians like Pelosi, Obama, Waters, Clinton, and others have helped push forward policies and legislative initiatives aligned with woke principles. However, their engagement with these ideas has also sparked significant resistance, contributing to cultural and political conflicts over the role of government, individual rights, and social justice in American life.

General Public Response to the Use of Woke by Politicians

The public response to the use of the term woke by politicians is highly polarized and varies widely depending on political alignment.

Many conservatives view the term woke as representative of overreach by progressives, aligning with their concerns over political correctness, cancel culture, and the perceived erosion of traditional values. For these individuals, politicians' use of the term is seen as a way to push back against what they consider unnecessary or divisive social agendas.

Progressives and those who advocate for social justice generally criticize the use of woke as a derogatory term. They argue that it undermines efforts to address systemic inequities and social injustices and that it is used by politicians to dismiss legitimate calls for reform. Many see it as a tactic to rile up the conservative base without engaging in meaningful policy discussions.

The term woke has also been widely satirized and parodied in popular culture. It is often the subject of memes, jokes, and debates across social media, reflecting its contested meaning and the cultural divide it represents. Both supporters and critics use humor to mock the perceived extremes of the other side's stance on wokeness.

Polarization and Division

The frequent use of the term woke by politicians has contributed to its polarization. For many, it has become shorthand for broader cultural battles over race, gender, history, and identity. This has led to deeper divisions, with each side often accusing the other of misrepresenting or misunderstanding what woke actually signifies.

Among younger generations, particularly Millennials and Gen Z, the term woke can have varying connotations. While some embrace it as a positive attribute associated with social awareness and justice, others may see it as overused or co-opted, losing its original meaning. Politicians' use of the term can sometimes come across as out of touch or pandering, especially when it seems disconnected from authentic advocacy for social change. The term woke has become a cultural and political flashpoint, used by politicians to either criticize or uphold social justice movements, with public responses reflecting the deepening ideological divides in society.

Chapter 4

Woke Ideologies in the Business Community

The term woke has also found its way into business environments, where it has been used by business owners and managers in various contexts, sometimes to embrace social justice principles and diversity initiatives, and at other times to criticize or push back against them. Let's consider some notable examples of how business leaders have used the term woke and how employees have responded:

Elon Musk (CEO of Tesla and X, formerly Twitter)

Elon Musk has frequently criticized woke culture. He has referred to wokeness as a mind virus that he believes is divisive and counterproductive. After acquiring Twitter in 2022, Musk used the platform to expose what he sees as excessive wokeness in media and technology sectors. He also made several management decisions, such as removing content moderation teams and reinstating previously banned accounts, which he framed as moves against woke censorship.

Musk's stance on wokeness has polarized employees. Some at Twitter (now X) and Tesla have welcomed his directness and agree with his criticism of political correctness, while others have resigned or spoken out against his leadership style and approach to sensitive social and political issues. Employees have raised concerns about a hostile work environment, and some have claimed that Musk's rhetoric and actions have created uncertainty and fear among workers, particularly those from marginalized communities.

Gary Kelly (Former CEO of Southwest Airlines)

Gary Kelly has discussed the company's approach to social issues in interviews, framing Southwest Airlines' culture as avoiding woke politics in favor of focusing on customer service and employee satisfaction. Kelly has indicated that Southwest does not want to take divisive public stances, suggesting that remaining neutral on politically charged issues is better for business.

The response from employees has been mixed. Some employees appreciate the company's focus on work culture and customer service over public political statements, feeling that it helps maintain a positive workplace environment. Others, however, believe that the company's neutrality can be interpreted as a lack of support for diversity and inclusion initiatives, leading to calls for clearer stances on social justice issues, especially from employees who belong to marginalized communities.

Goya Foods (Robert Unanue, CEO)

In 2020, Goya Foods CEO Robert Unanue publicly praised then-President Donald Trump, leading to a backlash from some consumers and employees who viewed Trump's policies as counter to social justice principles. In response to the criticism, Unanue doubled down, describing those who called for boycotts as woke activists trying to cancel anyone who disagreed with them.

Employees and consumers were divided by Unanue's remarks. Some employees, particularly those who disagreed with his political stance, felt alienated and expressed discomfort with the CEO's rhetoric. Others felt supported, particularly those who shared Unanue's political views. The controversy also sparked calls for greater transparency about the company's values and corporate social responsibility.

Brian Armstrong (CEO of Coinbase)

In 2020, Brian Armstrong published a blog post stating that the company would not engage in social or political activism unrelated to its core mission, framing this decision as a rejection of woke corporate culture. Armstrong offered severance packages to employees who disagreed with this stance and wanted to leave the company.

Armstrong's statement led to the departure of about 5% of Coinbase employees, who felt that the company was shutting down discussions on important social issues. However, some remaining employees and supporters viewed the move as a necessary focus on the company's core mission and an effort to prevent distractions from political debates. The incident sparked broader discussions about the role of businesses in social and political activism.

Basecamp (Jason Fried and David Heinemeier Hansson, Co-founders)

In 2021, Basecamp co-founders Jason Fried and David Heinemeier Hansson announced that the company would no longer allow societal and political discussions on its internal communication platforms, describing these debates as unproductive and a distraction from the company's work. This move was seen as a reaction against woke culture and the perceived pressure to conform to certain social and political viewpoints within the workplace.

The announcement led to significant pushback from Basecamp employees, with about a third of the company's workforce resigning in protest. Many employees felt that the new policy silenced important discussions and ignored the realities of systemic issues that affect their daily lives and work. Some employees criticized the decision as failing to provide a safe and inclusive workplace, while others supported the idea of focusing solely on work.

Support for Neutrality or Anti-Woke Stance

Some employees appreciate it when their employers avoid woke politics or social activism, feeling that it helps to maintain a neutral and focused work environment. They may support policies that prioritize business goals over social and political debates, especially if they feel these debates are polarizing or distracting from the company's mission.

In many cases, employees have pushed back against anti-woke stances, particularly when they perceive these stances as dismissive of diversity, equity, and inclusion (DEI) efforts. Employees who are passionate about social justice issues may view such rhetoric as undermining their values and making the workplace less inclusive. This has sometimes led to resignations, public critiques, or internal advocacy for policy changes.

Employees who disagree with anti-woke rhetoric often call for more inclusive practices and greater support for marginalized groups within the company. This can include advocating for DEI initiatives, employee resource groups, and more open dialogues about social issues. They may argue that diversity and inclusion are essential for both ethical and business reasons.

Concern Over Corporate Culture and Reputation

The use of woke terminology by business leaders can also lead to polarization within the workplace, with employees feeling divided along ideological lines. This can create tension and conflict among staff, affecting morale and potentially impacting productivity.

Employees may also be concerned about how a company's stance on woke issues affects its external reputation, recruitment, and retention efforts. In competitive industries, companies perceived as hostile to social justice or diversity initiatives may struggle to attract diverse talent or appeal to socially conscious consumers. Overall, how employees respond to their employer's use of the term woke largely depends on their individual values, the company's culture, and the context in which the term is used.

Companies' and business management's implementation of woke policies can significantly affect their customer base, revenue streams, and overall profitability, often in polarizing ways. When a company aligns itself with or against woke ideologies—either by supporting or rejecting social justice movements—it can attract certain customer demographics while alienating others. Now let's take a look at five examples of how the use of the term woke by companies or business leaders has impacted their financial and market performance:

Bud Light (Anheuser-Busch InBev)

In April 2023, Bud Light collaborated with transgender influencer Dylan Mulvaney to celebrate his "365 Days of Girlhood," creating a personalized beer can featuring her image. This marketing move was perceived by some as a woke stance in support of LGBTQ+ issues.

The campaign sparked a backlash among some conservative consumers who perceived the brand as pushing a woke agenda. Calls for boycotts circulated widely on social media, leading to a significant drop in sales. Reports indicated that Bud Light's U.S. sales fell by more than 25% in the weeks following the controversy, and Anheuser-Busch InBev's stock value took a hit. However, the company's stance also garnered support from progressive consumers, leading to a polarized customer base.

While the boycott negatively impacted short-term revenue and brand perception among conservative consumers, the long-term profitability effects are still undecided. The incident demonstrated the risks of engaging in polarizing social issues, where attempts to align with social justice movements could lead to a backlash from other segments.

Disney

In 2022, Disney CEO Bob Chapek faced controversy over the company's response to Florida's Parental Rights in Education bill, labeled by critics as the "Don't Say Gay" bill. After initial silence, Disney publicly opposed the bill, a move that many saw as embracing a woke position on LGBTQ+ rights. In response, Florida Governor Ron DeSantis accused Disney of promoting a woke agenda and moved to strip the company of its self-governing status in the state.

Disney's decision polarized its customer base. Some conservative customers criticized the company for getting involved in politics, leading to boycotts and public campaigns against Disney products and services. Meanwhile, progressive customers and LGBTQ+ advocacy groups praised Disney's stance.

Although Disney faced some backlash and political challenges, the financial impact was mitigated somewhat by its strong brand loyalty and diversified revenue streams. However, the ongoing conflict with Florida's government could have long-term implications for its operations, particularly in its theme parks, which are a major source of revenue.

Chick-fil-A

Chick-fil-A, a fast-food chain, has faced repeated criticism for its CEO and company's support of organizations opposing same-sex marriage, a stance viewed as anti-woke. The company was widely associated with socially conservative values, which led to boycotts by LGBTQ+ groups and allies.

The controversy led to mixed effects on Chick-fil-A's customer base. Some progressive consumers boycotted the chain, while many conservative customers rallied around it, leading to increased sales in certain regions. In fact, Chick-fil-A's revenue continued to grow in conservative markets, highlighting its appeal to a specific customer segment.

Despite the boycotts, Chick-fil-A has remained highly profitable and continued to expand. Its focus on customer service, quality, and operational efficiency has helped mitigate the negative impact of any backlash. However, the controversy shows that taking a stance on social issues can solidify loyalty among certain consumers while alienating others.

Gillette (Procter & Gamble)

In 2019, Gillette released an ad campaign titled "The Best Men Can Be," which tackled toxic masculinity and encouraged men to challenge harmful behaviors. The campaign was viewed as a woke message by many, sparking both praise and backlash. Some consumers accused Gillette of virtue signaling and promoting woke ideals, leading to calls for boycotts.

The campaign generated significant controversy and led to a polarized response. While some applauded Gillette for promoting social responsibility, others felt alienated and boycotted the brand, resulting in a reported $8 billion write-down for Procter & Gamble. The company claimed that the campaign was successful in terms of engagement and reaching younger audiences but acknowledged that it came with some financial costs.

The immediate financial impact included both a hit to sales and a loss in market value. However, the brand argued that it successfully increased awareness and visibility among younger consumers, which could potentially have positive long-term effects. The case illustrates the risk-reward balance companies face when aligning with woke social causes.

MyPillow (Mike Lindell, CEO)

MyPillow CEO Mike Lindell, a staunch supporter of Donald Trump, has frequently criticized woke culture and has used his platform to promote conservative political views, particularly in relation to election fraud claims following the 2020 U.S. Presidential Election.

Lindell's strong political stances led to several major retailers, such as Bed Bath & Beyond and Kohl's, dropping MyPillow products from their stores. This resulted in a significant decrease in the company's revenue. However, Lindell leveraged his anti-woke stance to appeal directly to conservative consumers, selling products through his own channels and bolstering sales by appealing to a specific customer demographic.

While MyPillow faced substantial revenue losses from traditional retail channels, it gained direct sales from a loyal, conservative customer base. The company's financial health became more dependent on Lindell's public persona and political alignment, showing that embracing an anti-woke stance can lead to short-term losses but can also foster niche market loyalty.

Companies that take a stance for or against woke culture often see their customer base split along ideological lines. This polarization can lead to increased loyalty from one group while alienating others, impacting sales in specific markets or demographics.

Engaging in woke or anti-woke messaging often leads to short-term revenue fluctuations due to boycotts or heightened brand engagement. Companies may see a dip in sales among those who oppose their stance but might also experience a boost from customers who support their position.

The impact on overall profitability depends on how well the company manages the controversy and whether it aligns with its core brand values. Businesses that effectively communicate their values while balancing diverse customer expectations may retain profitability, while those perceived as inconsistent, or alienating may face longer-term challenges.

Companies engaging in woke or anti-woke messaging face heightened scrutiny from both customers and the public, requiring careful management of public relations to maintain a positive reputation and brand image.

Companies may strategically decide to position themselves within a specific market segment, using woke or anti-woke rhetoric to solidify loyalty among targeted demographics, which can ultimately impact their long-term business strategy and growth potential.

Overall, how businesses navigate the use of woke rhetoric significantly impacts their market performance and balance sheet, reflecting the complex interplay between corporate values, customer preferences, and social and political dynamics.

Chapter 5

The Correlation Between Woke Ideologies and DEI Ideologies

In recent years, two terms—woke and DEI—have become central to discussions around social justice, workplace culture, and broader societal change. While these terms are often used in similar contexts, they have distinct origins, meanings, and applications. Understanding the correlation between woke ideologies and DEI (Diversity, Equity, and Inclusion) ideologies requires defining each and examining how they intersect and diverge in their goals, practices, and impacts.

Defining Woke

The term woke originated in African American Vernacular English (AAVE) in the early 20th century, meaning to be "awake" or aware, particularly regarding social injustice and systemic oppression. In its contemporary context, woke refers to a heightened awareness of social inequalities and a commitment to challenging and rectifying those injustices, particularly around race, gender, sexuality, and other marginalized identities.

Being woke involves recognizing the ways that societal structures, institutions, and cultural norms perpetuate discrimination and inequality. This ideology emphasizes activism, allyship, and advocacy for marginalized groups. It calls for individuals and communities to be alert to social injustice and to work actively against various forms of systemic oppression. However, the term has also been politicized and used pejoratively by critics to describe what they see as excessive political correctness or radical progressivism.

Defining DEI

DEI stands for Diversity, Equity, and Inclusion. This framework is primarily applied within organizational and institutional contexts, such as workplaces, schools, and governmental bodies, to create environments that are more inclusive and representative of diverse identities.

Diversity refers to the presence of differences within a given setting. This can include differences in race, ethnicity, gender, age, sexual orientation, disability, socioeconomic status, religion, and other attributes.

Equity focuses on fairness and justice, aiming to ensure that policies, practices, and systems do not disadvantage certain groups. It involves providing different levels of support and resources to ensure that everyone has equal access to opportunities.

Inclusion is about creating environments where all individuals feel welcomed, respected, and valued. It goes beyond diversity by ensuring that everyone, regardless of their background, has a sense of belonging and can fully participate in organizational or community life.

DEI ideologies advocate for systemic changes to promote fairness and inclusivity within organizations. This can involve implementing policies that combat discrimination, offering training and development on unconscious bias, ensuring equal pay, and creating supportive environments for underrepresented groups.

The Correlation Between Woke and DEI Ideologies

While woke and DEI ideologies are distinct, they are closely related and often intersect in their goals of challenging injustice and promoting equality.

At their core, both woke and DEI ideologies aim to address social inequalities and promote justice. Woke ideology calls for awareness and action against systemic injustices in all areas of society, from policing to housing, while DEI specifically targets organizational structures and practices to ensure fairness and inclusivity. The underlying belief is that everyone, regardless of background or identity, should have equal access to opportunities, resources, and treatment.

Both ideologies recognize the existence of biases—whether conscious or unconscious—that perpetuate inequality. Woke ideology emphasizes the importance of recognizing one's own biases and the ways in which they contribute to systemic injustice. It often involves advocating for changes in laws, social norms, and behaviors to dismantle these biases.

Similarly, DEI efforts focus on identifying and mitigating biases within organizational settings. This could involve revising hiring practices to be more inclusive, conducting regular bias training for employees, or creating policies that address discrimination and harassment. Both approaches understand bias as a fundamental barrier to equality that must be actively addressed.

Both ideologies advocate for the rights and well-being of marginalized groups, although their strategies may differ. Woke ideology often involves grassroots activism, protests, public campaigns, and calls for broad societal change. It may involve challenging dominant narratives, holding institutions accountable, and demanding reforms in public policies.

DEI efforts, on the other hand, are more focused on creating change within specific institutions. They often involve setting measurable goals, such as increasing representation of underrepresented groups in leadership positions or closing pay gaps and implementing policies that foster a more inclusive culture.

Both woke and DEI ideologies promote the use of inclusive language and practices to challenge harmful stereotypes and foster a culture of respect. For example, they both encourage using gender-neutral language, recognizing diverse cultural holidays, and being mindful of how different forms of communication can affect marginalized groups.

In workplaces, DEI initiatives may involve changing company policies to reflect these inclusive practices, while woke culture might emphasize the personal responsibility of individuals to use language that is respectful and affirming of diverse identities.

Differences Between Woke and DEI Ideologies

While woke and DEI ideologies share common goals, they differ in their methods, contexts, and scope. Woke ideology is broad and encompasses all areas of social life, often focusing on broader systemic changes beyond organizational boundaries. It may advocate for significant reforms in areas such as law enforcement, healthcare, and education.

DEI ideology is more targeted, primarily focused on creating equitable and inclusive environments within specific organizations or institutions. It is often driven by policy changes, training programs, and strategic initiatives that aim to foster a culture of inclusivity.

Woke ideology often employs grassroots activism, protests, and social media campaigns to raise awareness and pressure institutions to change. It can be confrontational and public facing, seeking to challenge and disrupt existing power structures.

DEI initiatives typically work from within organizations, using data-driven approaches, policy changes, and leadership development programs. They focus on gradual, systemic changes that align with the organization's values and objectives.

The term woke has become highly politicized, with supporters viewing it as a necessary stance for justice and critics arguing that it represents excessive political correctness or "cancel culture." This polarization can sometimes overshadow the substantive goals of social justice.

DEI, while also facing criticism, especially from those who see it as an imposition of ideology, is often perceived as more neutral and institutional. It is framed as a strategic business or organizational initiative, supported by data on employee satisfaction, retention, and performance.

To recap, woke and DEI ideologies are closely correlated in their emphasis on challenging social injustice and promoting equality. They share common goals of advocating for marginalized groups, addressing biases, and creating inclusive environments. However, they differ in their scope, methods, and the contexts in which they operate.

Woke ideology is a broader cultural movement that calls for systemic change and social awareness on a wide range of issues, while DEI initiatives are more focused efforts within organizations to create fair and inclusive workplaces. Both play critical roles in advancing social justice, but they operate on different levels, one in the realm of public discourse and activism, and the other within organizational and institutional frameworks.

Chapter 6

Diversity, Equity, and Inclusion vs Affirmative Action

Diversity, Equity, and Inclusion (DEI) mandates and Affirmative Action policies are both designed to address social inequalities and promote fair treatment within the workplace and educational settings. While they share some common goals, they differ significantly in their scope, methods, and historical context. Each has had a distinct economic and cultural impact on the business community and American society as a whole.

Both DEI mandates and Affirmative Action policies aim to promote equality by addressing disparities and reducing discrimination against historically marginalized groups, including racial minorities, women, and people with disabilities. They share a commitment to creating opportunities for underrepresented groups to participate fully in workplaces, educational institutions, and other societal settings.

Both DEI and Affirmative Action policies emphasize increasing the representation of historically marginalized groups. Affirmative Action explicitly focuses on improving access to employment and education for these groups, while DEI goes further by aiming to create an inclusive culture where everyone feels valued and respected. They both promote practices such as targeted recruitment, scholarships, mentorship programs, and support systems for underrepresented groups.

Basis in Legal and Social Justice Frameworks

Affirmative Action policies were enacted as part of civil rights legislation in the 1960s to rectify the historical injustices of segregation and systemic discrimination. Similarly, DEI initiatives are often grounded in legal frameworks, such as anti-discrimination laws, and social justice principles advocating for fairness and equality. Both approaches are based on the idea that deliberate actions by the federal government are necessary to level the playing field and create opportunities for those who have been historically disadvantaged.

Differences Between DEI and Affirmative Action

Affirmative Action is a set of policies and practices designed to increase opportunities for historically marginalized groups, specifically in areas like employment, government contracting, and college admissions. Affirmative Action often involves quotas or specific targets to increase representation of these groups and was initially focused on racial and gender minorities.

DEI Mandates are broader in scope. While Affirmative Action focuses on improving access and representation, DEI goes beyond representation to address equity (fair treatment, access, and advancement) and inclusion (creating environments where all individuals feel respected, valued, and able to contribute). DEI also includes a wider range of identities, such as LGBTQ+ individuals, people with disabilities, and those from diverse socioeconomic backgrounds. It incorporates training, policy changes, leadership development, and cultural transformation within organizations.

Affirmative Action often involves legally mandated policies, such as specific hiring or admission practices, set quotas or goals, and compliance with federal or state regulations. It includes measures like race-conscious hiring practices, which were often enforced by government oversight or judicial rulings.

DEI Mandates were originally intended to be voluntary programs and initiatives adopted by organizations to foster a more inclusive culture. They are not always legally required and are often driven by a company's internal goals, values, or market pressures. DEI strategies might include implicit bias training, employee resource groups, mentorship programs, and changes to workplace policies that support a more inclusive environment.

Affirmative Action is seen as a corrective measure, directly addressing past discrimination by taking steps to balance the scales through legally defined practices. It often focuses on quantitative outcomes (e.g., percentage of minority hires or admissions).

DEI Mandates represent a more holistic approach, aimed at changing organizational culture to be more inclusive and equitable in the long term. They emphasize qualitative outcomes, such as employee engagement, belonging, and psychological safety, in addition to diversity metrics.

Affirmative Action has helped businesses tap into a broader range of talent by mandating the inclusion of diverse candidates. Theoretically this has contributed to increased innovation and creativity, as diverse teams are often better at problem-solving and decision-making. Companies with diverse workforces have been better positioned to understand and reach diverse customer bases, which can enhance market share and profitability.

Implementing Affirmative Action policies required businesses to invest in government mandated compliance systems, training, and administrative processes to ensure adherence to regulations, which sometimes increased operational costs.

Affirmative Action faced significant political and legal pushback. Critics argued it invariably results in "reverse discrimination" or preferential treatment based on race or gender rather than merit. This led to lawsuits and legal battles, such as the U.S. Supreme Court's decision in Regents of the University of California v. Bakke (1978), which ruled against racial quotas.

Historically, research has shown that employees who feel included and valued are more engaged, productive, and likely to stay with a company. This can reduce turnover costs and increase overall productivity.

Diverse and inclusive teams tend to be more innovative, better at identifying and addressing a wide range of market needs, and more effective in making decisions. Companies with strong DEI practices are often perceived as more adaptable and resilient, which can enhance long-term profitability. Similarly, companies that embrace DEI tend to have stronger reputations as socially responsible businesses, which can attract customers, investors, and employees who value inclusivity over skill and qualification.

DEI initiatives often require significant investment in training, policy development, data collection, and strategy. These costs can be substantial, especially for smaller organizations without dedicated resources.

Conversely, DEI programs often face resistance from employees, stakeholders, or the public, particularly when perceived as politically driven or overly prescriptive. This can lead to internal conflict, reduced morale, or public relations challenges.

Economic and Cultural Impact on American Society

Affirmative Action played a crucial role in advancing civil rights in the U.S., breaking down barriers to employment and education for marginalized groups. It reshaped the American workplace and educational institutions, making them more reflective of the country's demographic diversity. It also sparked ongoing debates about fairness, meritocracy, and the role of government in addressing social inequalities, which continue to influence public policy and discourse.

Affirmative Action has contributed to the growth of a diverse middle class and increased economic mobility for minorities and women. By providing greater access to education and employment opportunities, it has helped reduce income disparities, although gaps remain.

Businesses that embraced Affirmative Action benefited from diverse talent pools and enhanced creativity, but some faced legal and administrative costs, and the broader economic impact has been mixed, depending on industry and region.

DEI initiatives have promoted a broader understanding of diversity beyond race and gender, encompassing a wide range of identities and fostering more inclusive environments in both corporate and social contexts.

DEI has also influenced American culture by encouraging discussions around privilege, unconscious bias, and systemic inequality. It has created new norms and expectations for what some claim to be a fairer and more inclusive workplace or institution.

A few companies with strong DEI practices have reported better financial performance, as diverse teams drive innovation and are more likely to capture new markets. Inclusive practices also reduce turnover costs and enhance employee satisfaction.

However, DEI efforts have also faced backlash, and many organizations struggle with the costs of implementation or resistance from those who view these initiatives as politically motivated or divisive.

Both Affirmative Action policies and DEI mandates aim to create a more equitable and just society by addressing historical and systemic inequalities. While Affirmative Action focuses on legally mandated access and representation for marginalized groups, DEI takes a broader, more holistic approach to foster inclusive environments and address a wide range of diversity dimensions.

The economic impact of each has been mixed, with benefits like access to diverse talent pools and improved innovation, balanced against challenges like compliance costs and resistance to mandates for hiring applicants based on their perceived identity rather than skill. Culturally, both have shaped American society by promoting equality and social justice, though they have also sparked debates about fairness, meritocracy, and the best methods to achieve a truly inclusive society.

Chapter 7

Benefits and Detriments of Incorporating Woke Ideology in Business

In recent years, many large businesses have embraced woke ideology in their workplaces, seeking to align themselves with contemporary social justice movements and evolving societal values. Woke ideology, in this context, involves fostering awareness and action against social inequalities, advocating for marginalized groups, and implementing policies that promote diversity, equity, and inclusion. While adopting woke principles can offer substantial benefits, it also carries potential risks and challenges that can impact a company's workforce dynamics, brand perception, and profitability.

Enhanced Employee Engagement

By embracing woke principles, companies portray a commitment to creating a fair, inclusive, and equitable workplace. Employees who feel respected, valued, and included are generally more engaged and motivated, leading to higher productivity, lower turnover rates, and reduced recruitment costs.

When companies support social justice initiatives and prioritize diversity, they can attract a wider range of applicants from different backgrounds, who are often more passionate and aligned with the company's values. Millennials and Gen Z workers, in particular, tend to prefer workplaces that align with their social and ethical values, making woke companies more attractive to younger, socially conscious talent pools.

Woke ideology encourages diverse perspectives and voices, which can lead to more creative problem-solving and innovative ideas. Diverse teams bring a wider array of experiences and viewpoints, allowing companies to approach challenges from multiple angles and adapt more effectively to changing market conditions.

Inclusive workplace cultures foster psychological safety, where employees feel comfortable sharing ideas without fear of judgment or retribution. This openness can enhance collaboration, leading to new products, services, and processes that drive competitive advantage.

Strengthened Brand Reputation and Customer Loyalty

Companies that embrace woke principles often build stronger brand reputations as ethical and socially responsible businesses. This can resonate with customers who prefer to support brands that align with their values, enhancing customer loyalty and driving sales.

Positive brand perception can also extend to investors, partners, and other stakeholders, who may view socially responsible companies as less risky and more forward-thinking. This can improve investor confidence, potentially leading to higher stock valuations and access to capital.

Companies that are proactive in adopting woke ideologies and addressing social justice issues may mitigate risks associated with public backlash, boycotts, or reputational damage. By taking a clear stand on social issues, businesses can position themselves as leaders in corporate responsibility, potentially avoiding negative publicity and regulatory scrutiny. Being aligned with contemporary social movements can help companies avoid the pitfalls of being perceived as out-of-touch or regressive, which can damage brand equity and customer trust.

In a small town, being a business that actively supports social justice and inclusivity can differentiate the company from competitors. This unique positioning can attract customers who prioritize ethical and progressive values, creating a niche market that can lead to increased customer loyalty and sales. By championing woke principles, small-town businesses can position themselves as leaders in community development, setting a positive example for other local businesses and contributing to broader social change within the community.

However, incorporating woke ideology, emphasizing social justice, diversity, equity, and inclusion, into small-town businesses can be a complex and nuanced endeavor. Unlike large corporations with extensive resources and diverse customer bases, small-town businesses operate within more localized and often tightly knit communities. As such, the effects of adopting woke principles can differ significantly in this context. While there are potential benefits to embracing these values, there are also notable risks and challenges that small-town businesses may face.

Detriments of Incorporating Woke Ideology in the Workplace

As mentioned, embracing woke ideology can lead to backlash from various stakeholders, including employees, customers, and investors who may perceive these actions as overly political or ideologically driven. Some individuals may feel that woke initiatives prioritize certain groups over others, leading to accusations of reverse discrimination or unfairness.

In highly polarized political climates, aligning with woke ideologies can alienate a segment of the customer base or workforce who do not share these views. This could result in lost sales, reduced customer loyalty, or negative publicity, impacting profitability.

Implementing woke principles in the workplace can lead to resistance from employees who may feel uncomfortable with mandated changes or perceive them as coercive or unnecessary. For example, mandatory bias training, changes to language guidelines, or policies perceived as tokenistic can create resentment or morale issues among employees who feel their autonomy is being restricted.

Woke initiatives can also lead to cultural clashes within the workforce, especially if there is a perception that certain groups are receiving preferential treatment. This can create tensions, reduce collaboration, and foster a divided workplace culture.

While many consumers appreciate companies that stand for social justice, others may react negatively, leading to calls for boycotts or public campaigns against the business. For instance, when companies take public stands on divisive social issues, they may inadvertently alienate parts of their customer base, resulting in a loss of revenue.

If woke initiatives are perceived as inauthentic or merely performative, they can backfire, damaging the company's credibility and trustworthiness. For example, if a company promotes woke values publicly but fails to reflect these principles in its internal practices, such as fair wages, equal opportunity, or sustainability, it may face accusations of hypocrisy, leading to reputational damage.

Financial Costs of Implementation

Adopting woke ideologies often requires substantial financial investment in training programs, policy changes, and diversity initiatives. This includes costs related to unconscious bias training, implementing new hiring practices, developing inclusive marketing campaigns, or creating support structures for underrepresented groups.

Additionally, focusing on woke initiatives might divert resources and attention from other core business activities, potentially impacting productivity, operational efficiency, and profitability. If the financial costs outweigh the benefits, especially in the short term, companies may experience a negative impact on their bottom line.

In small towns where traditional values often prevail, adopting woke principles can lead to backlash from community members who view these initiatives as unnecessary or politically motivated. This resistance can manifest in negative publicity, reduced customer patronage, or strained relationships with local stakeholders. Businesses that champion progressive values might alienate local customers who disagree with these principles, leading to decreased sales and profitability. In small towns, where customer loyalty is often closely tied to community values, this can have a significant impact on the business.

Impact on Workforce and Profitability

Companies that successfully integrate woke ideologies can create a more inclusive, engaged, and motivated workforce. Employees who feel valued and supported are more likely to stay with the company, reducing turnover rates and fostering a positive work culture. However, if not managed carefully, woke initiatives can create tension, resistance, and division within the workforce. Employees who feel alienated or disagree with the company's stance may disengage, leading to lower productivity, higher turnover, and a potentially toxic work environment.

Companies that align with woke ideologies may see a positive impact on profitability through enhanced brand reputation, niche customer loyalty, and access to a diverse talent pool. Inclusive practices can lead to better decision-making, higher innovation, and greater market adaptability, contributing to long-term financial success.

Conversely, companies that face backlash, resistance, or reputational damage due to their woke stance often experience a decline in customer base, sales, and profitability. The costs associated with implementing woke policies, coupled with potential loss of market share, can negatively affect the bottom line, particularly if perceived as inauthentic or misaligned with customer values.

For small-town businesses, incorporating woke ideology involves a balancing act between embracing progressive values and managing the potential risks associated with such a shift. While there are perceived benefits such as enhanced employee satisfaction, differentiation in the market, and strengthened community relationships, there are also significant challenges, including potential backlash, resource constraints, and risks of perceived inauthenticity.

Ultimately, the impact of adopting woke ideology on a company's workforce and profitability depends on how authentically and strategically these principles are implemented. Companies that successfully integrate woke values with genuine commitment and thoughtful communication can position themselves as leaders in social responsibility and corporate ethics. Conversely, businesses that fail to balance these initiatives with their core values, stakeholder interests, and market realities may face significant challenges that could undermine their success.

The High Costs of Woke and DEI Policies

As of this writing, there is no specific data or comprehensive study indicating the exact number of companies that have declared bankruptcy solely due to implementing woke and DEI policies. The impact of adopting these policies on a company's financial stability can be complex and multifaceted, involving various factors beyond just DEI initiatives.

While implementing DEI policies can involve costs related to training, policy development, and hiring practices, these expenses alone are unlikely to drive a company into bankruptcy. More typically, bankruptcy results from a combination of financial mismanagement, customer alienation, declining revenues, or significant operational challenges.

Some companies may face backlash from consumers or communities due to perceived inauthenticity or political stances, potentially impacting their revenue. However, while such backlash might affect profitability, it is usually one of many factors that contribute to financial distress rather than the sole cause of bankruptcy.

The broader economic environment, including market conditions and industry-specific challenges, often plays a more significant role in a company's financial difficulties. In many cases, financial issues are the result of a combination of factors, including market competition, economic downturns, and internal mismanagement, rather than DEI policies alone.

Anecdotal Evidence

Some companies have faced public criticism or backlash related to their DEI initiatives, which may affect their brand reputation and customer base. For example, businesses might experience negative media coverage or consumer boycotts, but these issues are usually part of a larger set of challenges faced by the company.

Legal and Financial Challenges

In certain instances, companies have encountered legal disputes or financial difficulties related to their DEI practices. For example, disputes over affirmative action policies or discrimination lawsuits might affect a company's financial health. However, these are often part of broader legal and financial issues rather than direct causes of bankruptcy.

Overall Assessment

While there have been instances of companies facing challenges or backlash related to their DEI policies, attributing bankruptcy solely to these initiatives is difficult. Financial difficulties leading to bankruptcy typically involve a range of factors, including but not limited to operational inefficiencies, market conditions, financial management issues, and broader economic trends. For a more precise assessment, it would require detailed case studies and financial analyses of companies that have implemented DEI policies and subsequently faced bankruptcy to determine the extent to which these policies contributed to their financial downfall.

Chapter 8

How Woke Ideology Impacts the Public Education System

Woke ideologies, emphasizing social justice, diversity, equity, and inclusion, have had a significant impact on the public education system. These ideologies have influenced various aspects of education, from curriculum development and teaching practices to school policies and student experiences. The integration of woke principles into education has been both praised and criticized, reflecting a complex interplay of educational goals and societal values.

Woke ideologies have led to the incorporation of diverse perspectives and historical narratives into school curricula. This includes a greater focus on the contributions and experiences of marginalized groups, such as African Americans, Indigenous peoples, LGBTQ+ individuals, and women. For example, many schools have revised history and literature curricula to include more comprehensive accounts of racial and gender inequalities.

Educators are increasingly adopting culturally responsive teaching practices that recognize and value students' diverse backgrounds. This approach helps to create a more inclusive and engaging learning environment by connecting curriculum content to students' lived experiences.

Woke principles emphasize the importance of social and emotional learning, which helps students develop empathy, self-awareness, and interpersonal skills. SEL programs aim to address issues such as bullying, discrimination, and mental health, fostering a more supportive and equitable school environment. Schools have implemented anti-bullying and anti-discrimination programs that align with woke ideologies. These initiatives aim to create safer and more inclusive spaces for all students, regardless of their background.

Woke ideologies have driven efforts to provide additional support for students from marginalized backgrounds, such as increased access to resources, mentorship programs, and academic support services. This includes initiatives aimed at closing achievement gaps and addressing disparities in educational opportunities.

There has also been a push to reform disciplinary practices to ensure they are fair and equitable. This includes efforts to reduce disparities in school discipline that disproportionately affect students of color and those from lower-income families.

Criticisms and Challenges

The integration of woke ideologies into curricula has sparked debates and controversies. Some critics argue that certain curriculum changes may present a one-sided view of historical events or social issues, potentially leading to polarized opinions among students and parents. For example, the inclusion of critical race theory (CRT) in some curricula has been a contentious issue, with opponents claiming it promotes division and bias.

The implementation of DEI-focused curricula has led to disagreements among parents and community members. In some cases, this has resulted in heated school board meetings and public debates over what should be taught in schools.

The adoption of woke principles in education has become a focal point in broader cultural and political debates. Some view these changes as part of a broader "culture war" and argue that they can contribute to ideological polarization within communities. This can create divisions between those who support progressive educational reforms and those who oppose them.

Teachers and school administrators may face pressure or scrutiny regarding their approach to implementing woke principles. In highly polarized environments, educators might encounter challenges in balancing diverse viewpoints and maintaining a focus on educational objectives.

Critics argue that an excessive focus on DEI initiatives can divert resources and attention from other critical areas of education, such as academic performance and basic skills development. There are concerns that the emphasis on social justice may come at the expense of traditional academic priorities.

Relevant Examples

In 2021, California became the first state to mandate an ethnic studies course as a graduation requirement for high school students. This course is intended to provide students with a broader understanding of diverse cultural and historical perspectives, reflecting woke ideologies in education.

Many school districts across the U.S. have implemented social and emotional learning (SEL) programs to support students' mental health and emotional well-being. These programs align with woke principles by addressing issues related to equity, inclusion, and mental health support.

Controversies Over Critical Race Theory

CRT emerged in the late 1970s and early 1980s in American law schools, largely as a response to what some scholars saw as the limitations of the Civil Rights Movement. Foundational figures like Derrick Bell, Kimberlé Crenshaw, Richard Delgado, and Patricia Williams were dissatisfied with the slow pace of racial reform following the civil rights era and the limitations of liberal legal strategies that focused primarily on formal equality and colorblindness. They argued that deeper structural and systemic changes were necessary to address the roots of racial inequality.

Critical Race Theory (CRT) is an intellectual and legal framework that examines the ways in which race and racism intersect with politics, culture, and law. It argues that racism is not merely the result of individual prejudice or bias, but is embedded in legal systems and policies, social practices, and institutions in ways that perpetuate racial inequalities. CRT originated in the United States in the late 1970s and early 1980s among legal scholars, but it has since expanded to other disciplines such as education, sociology, and political science.

CRT claims that racism is a normal and enduring aspect of society, not an anomaly. It contends that racial inequalities are maintained through both overt and covert practices embedded in institutions, laws, and policies that advantage certain racial groups over others, particularly white people over people of color.

A key concept in CRT, introduced by legal scholar Derrick Bell, is the idea that advances in racial justice tend to occur only when they also serve the interests of white people. This concept suggests that true equity will not be achieved if it threatens the power or privilege of white people.

CRT maintains that race is not a biological or natural reality, but a social construct that has been created and manipulated over time to serve specific political, economic, and social goals. This view challenges the idea that racial categories are fixed and unchanging, emphasizing instead how they are fluid and shaped by societal forces.

Introduced by Kimberlé Crenshaw, a foundational CRT scholar, intersectionality is the idea that individuals can experience discrimination in multiple ways based on intersecting aspects of their identity, such as race, gender, class, sexual orientation, and more. CRT argues that these intersecting identities must be considered to understand the complexity of discrimination and social inequality.

CRT emphasizes the importance of counter-narratives or the stories and experiences of marginalized groups. It suggests that dominant cultural narratives often obscure or distort the lived realities of racial minorities. By highlighting these alternative perspectives, CRT aims to challenge dominant assumptions about race and racism.

Over time, CRT scholars began to critique mainstream legal approaches that relied on incremental change and that often failed to challenge the broader social and economic systems that perpetuated racial injustice. They contended that the law, rather than being neutral or objective, is a tool that has historically been used by white people to maintain the status quo and protect the interests of those in power.

Criticism and Controversy Surrounding Critical Race Theory

CRT has become highly controversial in recent years, especially as its principles have begun to be applied outside of academia, in areas such as education, workplace diversity training, and public policy. Critics argue that CRT promotes a divisive, negative view of society, emphasizing racial identity over individual merit, and undermines traditional liberal values such as equality and colorblindness. They claim that CRT encourages a form of "reverse racism" by positioning all white people as inherently privileged and complicit in oppression.

Promotion of Socialism by College and University Professors

Since the early twentieth century, colleges and universities in the United States and other parts of the world have served as significant platforms for the dissemination and promotion of socialist ideas. Professors, as key influencers in academia, have often used their positions to introduce, teach, and advocate for socialist thinking, encouraging critical examination of capitalist structures and fostering debates on alternative economic and social systems. Their efforts, shaped by historical events, cultural shifts, and intellectual movements, have played a vital role in integrating socialist perspectives into the broader educational and societal landscape.

The early 1900s marked a period of rapid industrialization, labor strife, and social upheaval in many parts of the world, including the United States and Europe. Against this backdrop, a number of university professors began to engage with socialist ideas, particularly Marxism, which provided a theoretical framework for understanding the economic inequalities and social injustices of the time.

Many scholars in disciplines such as economics, sociology, history, and political science began to incorporate Marxist analysis into their teaching and research. For example, in the 1920s and 1930s, economists and social scientists at institutions like Columbia University and the University of Chicago explored Marxist critiques of capitalism, examining how economic systems generated class conflict and perpetuated social inequalities. They introduced students to works by Karl Marx, Friedrich Engels, and other socialist thinkers, often framing these ideas as valuable tools for critiquing the existing social order.

The Russian Revolution of 1917 had a profound impact on global intellectual thought, inspiring a wave of interest in socialism and communism among academics. Professors at universities in the United States, the United Kingdom, Germany, and beyond began to engage more deeply with socialist ideas, viewing the revolution as a practical experiment in the implementation of Marxist theory. Scholars like John Dewey, an American philosopher and education reformer, debated the merits and shortcomings of the Soviet model, encouraging students to consider alternatives to capitalist democracy.

The mid-twentieth century was marked by intense ideological conflict between capitalism and socialism, most notably during the Cold War between the United States and the Soviet Union. During this period, many professors continued to teach and promote socialist thinking, often in defiance of anti-communist sentiment and political pressure.

During the 1950s, the rise of McCarthyism in the United States led to widespread suspicion and persecution of individuals believed to be associated with communism. Many university professors faced scrutiny, blacklisting, and even dismissal for their perceived leftist sympathies. Despite this hostile environment, some professors continued to promote socialist ideas covertly, using coded language or focusing on broader social justice themes that aligned with socialist principles. They fostered underground networks of intellectual discussion, often mentoring students who would go on to become leaders in social justice movements.

The 1960s and 1970s saw a resurgence of socialist thinking on college campuses, driven in part by the civil rights movement, the anti-Vietnam War protests, and other social justice causes. Professors like Howard Zinn, an American historian and social activist, openly challenged capitalist narratives and promoted socialist alternatives in their classrooms. Zinn's book, A People's History of the United States, for example, presented American history from the perspective of marginalized groups, critiquing the capitalist exploitation of labor and resources.

In addition, many professors became directly involved in activist movements, using their academic positions to organize protests, write radical pamphlets, and educate students about the connections between capitalism, imperialism, and social inequality. The New Left movement, which emerged during this time, saw many academics advocating for a combination of Marxist, socialist, and anarchist ideas, fostering a climate of radical thought on campuses across the Western world.

The late twentieth century witnessed the rise of critical theory, an intellectual movement that originated with the Frankfurt School of social theory in Germany and spread to American universities. Critical theory, heavily influenced by Marxism, sought to understand and critique the power dynamics underlying capitalist societies, including the ways in which culture, ideology, and institutions perpetuate domination and inequality.

Professors such as Herbert Marcuse, Theodor Adorno, and Max Horkheimer, affiliated with the Frankfurt School, moved to the United States and other Western countries to escape Nazi persecution. They took up positions in American universities and began to teach critical theory, incorporating Marxist concepts into the study of culture, society, and economics. This led to the development of fields like cultural studies, critical race theory, and feminist theory, which sought to analyze the intersections of capitalism, culture, and power.

During this period, many professors began to introduce concepts associated with cultural Marxism, which argued that cultural hegemony, the dominance of capitalist ideologies and values, served to maintain the existing social order. Professors in sociology, anthropology, literature, and political science departments explored how media, education, and popular culture reinforced capitalist norms and values, and encouraged students to think critically about how these systems might be challenged and reformed.

In the twenty-first century, a new wave of interest in socialist ideas has emerged on college campuses, driven by economic crises, growing inequality, and the rise of progressive social movements.

The financial crisis of 2008 and the subsequent economic recession reignited interest in socialist critiques of capitalism. Professors began to reintroduce and popularize socialist and Marxist ideas, emphasizing their relevance in understanding the failures of neoliberal capitalism. Scholars like Richard D. Wolff, a prominent Marxist economist, used their academic platforms to argue that capitalism is inherently unstable and to advocate for alternative models, such as democratic socialism.

The resurgence of social justice movements, such as Black Lives Matter and environmental activism, has also led many professors to promote socialist ideas. These movements often call for systemic change to address the deep-rooted inequalities perpetuated by capitalist structures. Professors across disciplines—from sociology to environmental science—have incorporated discussions of socialism into their curricula, framing it as a necessary consideration in debates about climate justice, racial equality, and economic redistribution.

With the rise of political figures like Bernie Sanders and Alexandria Ocasio-Cortez, who identify as democratic socialists, the term "socialism" has entered mainstream political discourse in new ways. College professors have often aligned with this movement, encouraging students to explore democratic socialism as a legitimate and viable alternative to neoliberal capitalism. Many professors actively participate in or support organizations like the Democratic Socialists of America (DSA), using their academic influence to promote policies such as universal healthcare, free college tuition, and workers' rights.

The Role of Universities as Incubators of Socialist Thought

Universities have historically been seen as incubators of radical and progressive ideas. They provide a space for intellectual freedom and critical thought, allowing professors to engage with and promote ideas that challenge the status quo. The tradition of academic freedom has allowed professors to explore socialist ideas without fear of censorship or reprisal. Tenure, a system that grants job security to professors, has further protected those who wish to teach and advocate for socialism. This institutional protection has enabled professors to discuss, debate, and promote socialist thought, fostering an environment where students are encouraged to critically engage with various ideologies.

Professors have often played a crucial role in nurturing student activism. Through lectures, seminars, and campus organizations, they have inspired generations of students to question existing social and economic systems and to consider socialist alternatives. This has contributed to a vibrant culture of student activism, where discussions about socialism, capitalism, and alternative economic models are a regular part of campus life.

From the early twentieth century to the present, college and university professors have been pivotal in promoting socialist thinking. Through their teaching, research, and activism, they have challenged dominant capitalist narratives and provided students with alternative frameworks for understanding society. Their efforts have shaped intellectual thought, fostered critical engagement with social and economic issues, and inspired new generations to consider socialism as a pathway to a more equitable and just society.

The impact of woke ideologies on the public education system has been significant, shaping curricula, teaching practices, and school policies. While these ideologies have led to positive changes in terms of inclusivity and support for marginalized students, they have also sparked controversies and challenges. The integration of woke principles into education reflects broader societal shifts and underscores the ongoing debates about the role of social justice in shaping educational experiences and outcomes.

Chapter 9

How Woke Ideology Has Impacted the Law Enforcement Agencies and Their Ability to Enforce the Law and Ensure Public Safety

The impact of woke ideologies on law enforcement agencies has been significant, influencing various aspects of policing, including policies, training, community relations, and public perceptions. Woke ideologies, which emphasize social justice, equity, and inclusion, have led to both positive reforms and contentious debates within the field of law enforcement. This chapter is a detailed examination of these impacts, including relevant examples.

Woke ideologies have driven efforts to reform use-of-force policies to ensure they are more just and equitable. For example, many police departments have adopted stricter guidelines on the use of lethal force, emphasizing de-escalation techniques and alternatives to violence. This is intended to reduce the number of fatal encounters between police and civilians, particularly in marginalized communities.

Law enforcement agencies have increasingly implemented training programs focused on implicit bias, cultural competency, and de-escalation. These programs aim to address systemic biases and improve interactions between officers and diverse communities. For instance, some departments have introduced crisis intervention training to better handle situations involving individuals with mental health issues.

The push for greater accountability has led to the widespread adoption of body-worn cameras by police officers. This technology provides a record of interactions between law enforcement and the public, which can enhance transparency and accountability. Additionally, there has been an increase in data reporting on police activities, including use-of-force incidents and demographic information, to monitor and address potential disparities.

Many communities have established civilian oversight boards or commissions to review police conduct and ensure accountability. These boards are designed to provide independent scrutiny of law enforcement practices and address concerns raised by community members.

Woke ideologies have emphasized the importance of community policing, which seeks to build positive relationships between law enforcement and the communities they serve. This approach involves officers working closely with community members to address local issues and foster trust. For example, community policing initiatives may include officers participating in neighborhood events, outreach programs, and collaborative problem-solving efforts.

Efforts to address systemic inequities have led to policies aimed at reducing racial profiling and discriminatory practices. Law enforcement agencies are increasingly scrutinizing arrest and stop-and-frisk data to identify and address patterns of racial bias. Additionally, there is a growing emphasis on ensuring that law enforcement practices are equitable and do not disproportionately impact marginalized communities.

Erosion of Law Enforcement Authority

Critics argue that some reforms associated with woke ideologies, such as reduced use of force or increased oversight, may undermine law enforcement authority and effectiveness. For example, there have been concerns that restrictions on the use of force could limit officers' ability to respond effectively to dangerous situations, potentially compromising public safety.

Some law enforcement professionals may resist or feel conflicted about changes associated with woke ideologies, viewing them as infringing on their ability to perform their duties effectively. This resistance can create tensions within police departments and impact morale.

The increased scrutiny and criticism of policing practices have led to heightened public and media attention on law enforcement agencies. This scrutiny can affect officer morale and contribute to a challenging working environment. Officers may feel that their actions are constantly under review, leading to stress and reduced job satisfaction.

Agencies may face public relations challenges related to perceptions of bias or misconduct, even when efforts are made to address these issues. Negative media coverage or high-profile incidents can overshadow positive reforms and impact public trust in law enforcement.

Implementing reforms associated with woke ideologies, such as new training programs or technology upgrades, can be costly. Law enforcement agencies may face financial constraints that limit their ability to fully implement these changes. Additionally, there may be challenges in balancing reform efforts with other operational priorities. Ensuring consistent and effective implementation of reforms can be challenging, particularly in larger jurisdictions with diverse needs.

Agencies may struggle to standardize practices and ensure that all officers adhere to new policies and procedures.

Relevant Examples

The death of convicted drug user and dealer George Floyd in 2020, and the subsequent protests, led to significant reforms in the Minneapolis Police Department. The city council voted to ban chokeholds and neck restraints, implement body cameras for all officers, and create a civilian oversight board. These changes reflect the influence of woke ideologies on policing practices.

New York City has expanded its body-worn camera program as part of efforts to increase transparency and accountability in policing. The program aims to provide an objective record of police interactions and enhance public trust in law enforcement.

Proposition 47, passed in California in 2014, reclassified certain non-violent felonies as misdemeanors and aimed to reduce incarceration rates for low-level offenses. While not solely driven by woke ideologies, the measure reflects broader efforts to address systemic inequities within the criminal justice system.

Portland, Oregon has focused on community policing as part of its efforts to build trust and improve relations between law enforcement and local communities. This includes initiatives such as community outreach programs and collaborative problem-solving efforts.

Following allegations of discriminatory policing practices, the Baltimore Police Department entered into a consent decree with the U.S. Department of Justice. The decree mandates reforms aimed at addressing racial bias, improving police practices, and enhancing transparency.

The impact of woke ideologies on law enforcement has led to significant reforms aimed at improving accountability, transparency, and community relations. While these changes have the potential to enhance public trust and address systemic inequities, they also present challenges related to perceived effectiveness, public criticism, and resource constraints. The evolving landscape of policing reflects a complex interplay between the pursuit of social justice and the practical realities of law enforcement.

Chapter 10

Similarities Between Woke Ideology and Key Tenets of Socialism

Woke ideology, which emphasizes social justice, equity, and inclusion, shares several similarities with socialism, a political and economic system that advocates for collective ownership, economic equality, and the redistribution of resources. While the two concepts are distinct, woke ideology is primarily focused on cultural and social issues, and socialism is traditionally associated with economic systems, their overlap in values and goals has led to frequent comparisons. Understanding these similarities can help clarify the ways in which both frameworks seek to challenge existing power structures and promote a more equitable society.

At its core, woke ideology is concerned with addressing and rectifying social injustices, particularly those related to race, gender, sexual orientation, and class. It seeks to dismantle systemic inequalities that are perceived to disadvantage marginalized groups. Advocates of woke ideology push for policies and practices that promote diversity, equity, and inclusion, such as affirmative action, reparations for historical injustices, and the redistribution of resources to achieve social equity.

Socialism is fundamentally concerned with economic equality and social welfare. It promotes the idea that the means of production should be owned or regulated by the community as a whole, rather than by private individuals. Socialists advocate for the redistribution of wealth and resources to ensure that all members of society have access to basic needs such as education, healthcare, and housing. This economic egalitarianism aligns with the woke goal of reducing disparities and providing more equitable opportunities for all individuals.

Both woke ideology and socialism advocate for a more equitable distribution of resources, whether those resources are material wealth, as in the case of socialism, or social and cultural capital, as in the case of woke ideology. Both frameworks challenge the concentration of power and privilege in the hands of a few and call for systemic changes to achieve greater fairness and justice.

Woke ideology often critiques capitalism as a system that perpetuates social inequalities. Many woke activists argue that capitalism inherently privileges those who already have economic power and disadvantages marginalized groups, particularly along lines of race, gender, and class. They contend that capitalism, by prioritizing profit over people, reinforces systemic oppression and fails to address the needs of the most vulnerable in society. The call for reparative justice, such as compensating communities for historical wrongs or investing in underserved areas, reflects this critique.

Socialism directly critiques capitalism as an economic system that leads to class stratification, economic inequality, and the exploitation of labor. Socialists argue that capitalism concentrates wealth and power in the hands of a few, while the working majority suffers from inadequate wages, poor working conditions, and lack of access to essential services. Socialism seeks to replace or reform capitalism through public ownership of resources, wealth redistribution, and social welfare policies to ensure that everyone's basic needs are met.

Both woke ideology and socialism are critical of the existing capitalist system, though for slightly different reasons. Socialism focuses on the economic exploitation and inequality generated by capitalism, while woke ideology critiques the broader social inequities that intersect with and are perpetuated by capitalist structures. Both movements advocate for systemic changes to create a more just society.

Advocacy for Government Intervention and Regulation

Proponents of woke ideology often call for greater government intervention in addressing social injustices. This includes policies like affirmative action, anti-discrimination laws, diversity quotas, and increased funding for public services such as education and healthcare. Many woke advocates believe that only through robust government action can systemic biases be dismantled and equity be achieved.

Socialism advocates for a significant role of the government in managing the economy and redistributing wealth. This includes the nationalization of key industries, provision of universal healthcare, free or affordable education, and a comprehensive social safety net. Socialists argue that the state should actively work to ensure that all individuals have equal opportunities and access to resources, and that the market should be regulated to prevent exploitation and inequality.

Both woke ideology and socialism see a vital role for government intervention in correcting imbalances and promoting social and economic justice. While woke ideology primarily focuses on social policies and anti-discrimination measures, socialism emphasizes economic policies. However, both advocate for the state as an agent of change to promote fairness and reduce inequality.

Emphasis on Collective Responsibility and Social Solidarity

Woke ideology emphasizes collective responsibility in recognizing and rectifying social injustices. It promotes the idea that all members of society have a role to play in challenging systemic inequalities and creating a more inclusive culture. This involves calling out discrimination, advocating for marginalized groups, and supporting policies that promote equity and diversity. The concept of "allyship," where individuals who are not directly affected by certain forms of oppression support those who are, reflects this sense of collective duty.

Socialism is built on the principle of social solidarity, which holds that the well-being of individuals is interconnected with that of the community. Socialists believe that society should function as a collective unit where resources are shared, and everyone's needs are met. This idea of collective ownership and mutual aid is central to socialist thought and aligns with the emphasis on social cohesion and solidarity found in woke ideology.

Both woke ideology and socialism promote the idea that individuals have a collective responsibility to work towards a more just and equitable society. This sense of shared duty to challenge inequalities and support marginalized communities is a common thread between the two frameworks.

A key component of woke ideology is intersectionality—the understanding that various forms of social stratification, such as race, gender, class, and sexual orientation, do not exist separately but are interconnected and impact individuals in complex ways. Woke advocates argue for a holistic approach to justice that addresses multiple, overlapping forms of oppression.

Socialism traditionally focuses on class struggle and the economic divide between the working class and the capitalist class. However, many modern socialists incorporate intersectional approaches, recognizing that class struggles intersect with other forms of oppression, such as racism, sexism, and xenophobia. This multi-issue advocacy aligns with the intersectional lens of woke ideology.

Both woke ideology and modern socialism advocate for a comprehensive approach to social justice that takes into account multiple, intersecting forms of inequality. They recognize that various systems of oppression are interlinked and must be addressed simultaneously to create a fairer and more equitable society.

While woke ideology and socialism differ in their historical origins, primary focuses, and specific strategies, they share several underlying principles. Both seek to challenge and reform existing power structures, promote equity, and advocate for government intervention to achieve a more just society. Woke ideology emphasizes social and cultural reform, focusing on dismantling systemic inequalities related to identity, while socialism traditionally centers on economic reform and the redistribution of wealth. Despite these differences, their converging goals around justice and equity have made them frequent allies in broader political and social movements advocating for transformative change.

Chapter 11

Woke Ideology: The Latest Iteration of the Left's Effort to Transform the U.S. into a Socialist Nation

Over the past century, the political Left in the United States has consistently sought to challenge and transform the nation's socio-economic structures, often aiming to shift the country towards a more socialist model. These efforts have taken on various forms, from labor movements and civil rights campaigns to academic debates and political organizing.

In recent years, woke ideology has emerged as the latest iteration of this long-standing project, combining social justice activism with a critique of traditional capitalist frameworks. By advocating for cultural, economic, and political changes, proponents of woke ideology are seen by some as advancing the Left's ongoing ambition to reshape the United States into a more socialist-oriented nation.

Since the early 20th century, left-wing activists in the United States have pushed for systemic reforms to address perceived social and economic inequalities. Inspired by socialist and Marxist ideologies, these efforts initially focused on labor rights, wealth redistribution, and public ownership of key industries. Movements such as the labor strikes of the 1930s, the New Deal policies under Franklin D. Roosevelt, and the rise of socialist-leaning organizations sought to limit the power of capital, protect workers, and promote a more equitable society. Though these movements achieved significant reforms, they ultimately fell short of transforming the U.S. into a fully socialist nation.

In the mid-20th century, new avenues for left-wing activism emerged. The civil rights movement, anti-war protests, and feminist and

LGBTQ+ movements expanded the scope of leftist agendas beyond purely economic concerns to include broader social justice issues. While these movements were not always explicitly socialist, they often intersected with socialist ideas by challenging established power structures and advocating for systemic change.

Woke ideology began to gain prominence in the 2010s as an expansion of these earlier social justice movements. "Woke" initially referred to being aware of and sensitive to social injustices, particularly those related to race and identity. However, it quickly evolved into a broader cultural movement that combines progressive activism with a deep critique of existing social, economic, and political systems.

Proponents of woke ideology argue that the United States is built on systems of oppression that extend beyond just economic inequality. They identify racism, sexism, heteronormativity, ableism, and other forms of discrimination as systemic problems embedded in the fabric of American society. This movement calls for comprehensive reforms to dismantle these structures, advocating for policies such as reparations for historical injustices, the defunding or reform of police forces, gender parity in leadership roles, and robust protections for marginalized groups. These demands often include calls for greater government intervention and regulation, mirroring the traditional goals of socialism.

The Convergence of Woke Ideology and Socialist Goals

Woke ideology, while distinct in its cultural and social focus, overlaps significantly with the goals of socialism in several key areas. Much like socialism, woke ideology advocates for redistributing resources and power from historically privileged groups to those deemed marginalized or oppressed. This includes supporting progressive taxation, universal healthcare, student loan forgiveness, and free college tuition. Many woke activists call for reparations for historical injustices, which aligns with socialist demands for redress and economic justice.

Woke ideology often critiques capitalism as a system that perpetuates inequality, commodifies human relations, and privileges profit over people. Many woke proponents argue that capitalist structures reinforce systemic oppression along lines of race, gender, and class. This critique echoes socialist arguments that capitalism is inherently exploitative and must be reformed or dismantled to achieve a more just and equitable society.

Woke activists frequently call for expanded government intervention in the economy and society to address social injustices. This includes not only economic reforms but also policies that regulate and control speech, behavior, and institutional practices to ensure inclusivity and equity. This mirrors the socialist emphasis on government as an agent of social change and a mechanism for enforcing equality.

Woke ideology has gained traction in various institutions across the U.S., from universities and media to corporate boardrooms and government agencies. Many of these institutions have adopted

Diversity, Equity, and Inclusion (DEI) policies and initiatives that reflect key tenets of woke thinking, such as prioritizing diversity in hiring, mandating anti-racism training, and adopting inclusive language guidelines. While these efforts are often framed as necessary to create fairer workplaces and environments, critics argue that they represent a covert means of advancing socialist goals by embedding progressive values into the institutional fabric of American life.

Politically, woke ideology has found champions among progressive lawmakers and candidates who advocate for transformative policies at the national level. Figures like Bernie Sanders and Alexandria Ocasio-Cortez have embraced elements of woke rhetoric while advancing democratic socialist platforms that call for massive wealth redistribution, universal healthcare, free college tuition, and the Green New Deal.

These politicians often argue that systemic racism, sexism, and other forms of discrimination cannot be fully addressed without fundamentally restructuring the economic system. This convergence of woke ideology and socialist policy goals suggests that both are part of a broader effort to push the U.S. toward a more socialist-oriented future.

Woke ideology has also influenced public discourse, reshaping conversations around identity, privilege, and systemic injustice. Social media platforms and online activism have played a significant role in amplifying these ideas, normalizing concepts such as privilege checking, intersectionality, and social justice advocacy in everyday conversations. By framing social issues in terms of systemic oppression and collective responsibility, woke ideology encourages a critical examination of capitalism and promotes ideas traditionally associated with the Left.

This cultural shift has had a polarizing effect on American society. While many people, especially younger generations, have embraced woke ideas as necessary to address deep-rooted inequalities, others see it as an overreach that threatens free speech, individual rights, and traditional American values. Critics argue that woke ideology, much like previous efforts by the Left, aims to reshape society in ways that align with socialist principles—prioritizing collective equity over individual liberty and encouraging government intervention in nearly all aspects of life.

Challenges to Woke Ideology

As woke ideology has gained prominence, it has also faced significant resistance. Critics argue that it represents a form of cultural and ideological authoritarianism, where dissenting opinions are labeled as bigoted or regressive. They contend that woke policies—such as defunding the police, implementing speech codes, or mandating DEI training—reflect a broader agenda to undermine capitalism and promote a socialist model. Some fear that these efforts could lead to increased government control, higher taxes, reduced individual freedoms, and economic stagnation.

This backlash has been evident in various political and social arenas. For example, in recent years, several states have passed laws to restrict the teaching of certain aspects of critical race theory or social justice activism in public schools and universities. Similarly, some corporations and organizations that have adopted woke policies have faced consumer boycotts or backlash from employees who view these initiatives as overreaching or divisive.

Woke ideology represents the latest manifestation of the Left's efforts to transform the United States into a more socialist-oriented nation. By merging traditional social justice activism with a critique of capitalism and calls for systemic change, proponents of woke ideology seek to reshape American society, culture, and economics in ways that align with socialist principles.

While this movement has gained considerable traction, it also faces significant challenges and resistance, reflecting the ongoing tension between competing visions for the nation's future. As the battle over woke ideology continues, it remains a central point of contention in the broader debate over America's identity and direction in the 21st century.

The idea of transforming the United States into a socialist nation has been a topic of debate for over a century, with significant milestones achieved along the way. These milestones have included the establishment of social welfare programs, progressive taxation, and increased government intervention in certain sectors of the economy. However, despite these achievements, the U.S. remains fundamentally a capitalist country. For the nation to officially adopt socialism, further key developments would be necessary, encompassing profound changes to the political, economic, and social systems.

Over the past century, several significant milestones have been achieved that reflect a shift toward socialist principles. These milestones illustrate an evolving embrace of government intervention, wealth redistribution, and social welfare, all of which align, to varying degrees, with socialist ideals.

The Great Depression of the 1930s provided the backdrop for one of the earliest significant milestones toward a more socialist orientation. President Franklin D. Roosevelt's New Deal included a series of programs and policies aimed at providing economic relief, stimulating recovery, and reforming the financial system to prevent future crises. Key components, such as Social Security, unemployment insurance, and public works programs, represented a substantial expansion of government intervention in the economy and the establishment of a welfare state. These initiatives marked a critical shift toward the idea that the government has a role in providing a social safety net for its citizens.

In the 1960s, President Lyndon B. Johnson's "Great Society" initiatives expanded on New Deal policies, further embedding government responsibility for social welfare. Programs like Medicare and Medicaid, the War on Poverty, and federal funding for education and housing aimed to reduce poverty and inequality, reflecting principles of wealth redistribution and increased public provisioning of services. These initiatives deepened the government's involvement in key areas of American life, moving the nation closer to a mixed economy that integrates elements of socialism.

Over the years, the U.S. has implemented a progressive income tax system, where higher-income earners are taxed at a higher rate, a principle consistent with socialist policies aimed at reducing wealth inequality. Furthermore, various tax credits and subsidies, such as the Earned Income Tax Credit (EITC) and child tax credits, have been used to redistribute wealth and provide economic support to lower-income families.

Over the decades, the U.S. has expanded social welfare programs to provide support for a broad range of needs, including food assistance (Supplemental Nutrition Assistance Program, or SNAP), housing assistance, and healthcare for the poor and elderly (Medicaid and Medicare). These programs reflect an increasing recognition of the state's role in providing for the basic needs of its citizens, moving closer to the socialist ideal of public provisioning of essential services.

The establishment of labor protections, such as the right to unionize, the minimum wage, overtime pay, and workplace safety regulations, aligns with socialist principles of protecting workers' rights and ensuring fair compensation. Additionally, movements for a "living wage" and expanded labor rights continue to push the U.S. toward policies that challenge unregulated capitalism.

The Affordable Care Act (ACA), also known as "Obamacare," was a significant step toward expanding government involvement in healthcare. While not a fully socialized system, the ACA sought to increase access to healthcare through government-subsidized insurance marketplaces, expanded Medicaid, and regulations on insurance companies. This represented a move closer to the socialist principle of universal healthcare, although it fell short of the single-payer systems found in many socialist countries.

Despite these milestones, the United States remains fundamentally a capitalist nation with a market-driven economy. For the U.S. to officially become a socialist nation, several key developments would need to occur, involving structural changes to the economic, political, and social systems.

Where Are We Headed

A hallmark of socialism is the public ownership or nationalization of key industries, such as healthcare, education, energy, transportation, and finance. In a socialist U.S., the government would assume control over these sectors to ensure that they operate for the public good rather than for private profit. For example, nationalizing the healthcare system would involve transitioning to a single-payer model, where the government directly provides or heavily regulates all healthcare services.

Similarly, nationalizing utilities and energy companies would involve the government taking ownership and control to prioritize environmental sustainability and equitable access over corporate profits.

Another key development would be the establishment of universal basic services such as healthcare, education, housing, and transportation. This would involve ensuring that every citizen has access to essential services free of charge or at minimal cost. The current administration and Congress have made several efforts to move toward establishing universal basic services in the United States, including healthcare, education, housing, and transportation and universal basic income. These efforts are driven by a broader vision of social equity and economic security, aiming to provide all citizens with essential services regardless of income or background.

A socialist U.S. would expand public investment in these areas, eliminating private profit motives and ensuring that access to basic needs is not determined by market forces or individual wealth. This could involve significant public spending, government-run programs, and the elimination of private alternatives that charge fees for these services.

To move toward socialism, the U.S. would also need to implement policies that expand social ownership and workers' control over production. This could include encouraging or mandating worker cooperatives, where employees collectively own and manage their workplaces. It might also involve implementing profit-sharing schemes, expanding union rights, and requiring companies to have worker representation on their boards. This shift would aim to democratize the workplace and reduce income inequality by ensuring that profits and decision-making power are shared more equitably among workers.

A socialist transformation would likely involve implementing a job guarantee or universal basic income to eliminate unemployment and provide a safety net for all citizens. A job guarantee program would commit the government to provide employment to anyone willing and able to work, typically in public service or infrastructure projects. Alternatively, a UBI would provide every citizen with a regular, unconditional cash payment, ensuring a minimum standard of living regardless of employment status. These policies would aim to reduce poverty, stabilize incomes, and shift economic power away from employers toward workers.

Moving toward socialism would require more aggressive wealth and income redistribution policies than currently exist. This will involve higher progressive taxes on income, wealth, and inheritance, alongside measures like capital controls and wealth caps. Such policies would aim to limit the accumulation of wealth among a small elite class, excepting congression members and administration leadership, and use public revenues to fund universal services and social programs. Establishment of a wealth tax, increased corporate taxes, and closing tax loopholes for the wealthy would be essential steps in this process.

For the U.S. to become a socialist nation, constitutional and legal reforms would likely be necessary to align the political system with socialist principles. This could involve revising, suspending, or amending the Constitution to guarantee economic rights, such as the right to employment, healthcare, and housing. Legal reforms might also be needed to limit the influence of private money in politics, ensuring that government decisions are driven by public interest rather than corporate interests.

Achieving socialism in the U.S. would require a significant cultural and ideological shift among the American populace. For much of its history, the U.S. has been defined by a capitalist ethos that values individualism, competition, and private enterprise. Moving toward socialism would require changing these deeply ingrained cultural norms, fostering a collective mindset that prioritizes social welfare, equity, and public ownership over individual profit and private wealth. This shift could be promoted through education, media, and public discourse, aiming to build broad-based support for socialist policies.

The Road Ahead

While several milestones have been achieved, the transition to a fully socialist nation in the U.S. would face significant challenges. There is strong political, economic, and cultural resistance to such a shift. Many Americans view socialism with skepticism, rightfully associating it with authoritarian regimes or the loss of individual freedoms. Additionally, powerful vested interests, such as corporations, financial institutions, and wealthy elites, are likely to oppose any moves toward socialism, fearing the loss of their economic power and influence. Unless, of course, they are incentivized by the government.

However, there are also opportunities. Growing economic inequality, social unrest, climate change, and public dissatisfaction with existing political structures have created fertile ground for discussions about systemic change. Progressive movements, particularly among younger generations, show increasing support for socialist ideas, such as universal healthcare, climate justice, and wealth redistribution.

While significant milestones have been achieved toward incorporating socialist principles into American governance and society, the U.S. remains far from becoming a fully socialist nation. Key developments such as nationalizing industries, guaranteeing employment and basic income, expanding social ownership, and enacting constitutional reforms would be necessary to complete this transformation. Whether the U.S. will continue on this path depends on future political, economic, and cultural developments, as well as the ability of socialist advocates to build broad-based support for their vision of a more equitable and just society. As the nation stands at this crossroads, the debate over its future direction remains as vigorous and contentious as ever.